Espresso YOUR Self

Cup of Resilience

Hanna Olivas

Along With 10 Inspiring Authors

TABLE OF CONTENTS

INTRODUCTION

There's something profoundly comforting about a warm cup of coffee—it's familiar, energizing, and often shared in moments of reflection or connection. *Espresso Yourself: A Cup of Resilience* was born from that same spirit: a gathering of voices, a pause to breathe, and a space to share stories that stir the soul.

This anthology is a tribute to the strength of women—those who have stumbled, risen, and dared to keep moving forward. Within these pages, you'll find a rich blend of experiences: moments of loss and love, fear and faith, brokenness and bold new beginnings. These stories, poems, and reflections are not just personal—they are universal. They remind us that we are never alone in our struggles or our triumphs.

Each contributor brings her own flavor, offering insight, hope, and healing. Some voices whisper, others roar—but all carry the message that resilience lives within us. This is a book for anyone who's ever had to start over, hold on, or fight for her place in the world.

So, find a quiet moment. Pour your favorite brew. And as you read, may you feel seen, supported, and empowered to espresso yourself—fully and unapologetically.

Hanna Olivas

Founder and CEO of SHE RISES STUDIOS

https://www.linkedin.com/company/she-rises-studios/
https://www.facebook.com/sherisesstudios
https://www.instagram.com/sherisesstudios_llc/
www.SheRisesStudios.com

Author, Speaker, and Founder. Hanna was born and raised in Las Vegas, Nevada, and has paved her way to becoming one of the most influential women of 2022. Hanna is the co-founder of She Rises Studios and the founder of the Brave & Beautiful Blood Cancer Foundation. Her journey started in 2017 when she was first diagnosed with Multiple Myeloma, an incurable blood cancer. Now more than ever, her focus is to empower other women to become leaders because The Future is Female. She is currently traveling and speaking publicly to women to educate them on entrepreneurship, leadership, and owning the female power within.

Espresso Yourself: Cup of Resilience

By Hanna Olivas

There's something sacred about a hot cup of coffee.

The steam rises like a whisper of hope in the early morning stillness. The warmth wraps around your hands like an old friend reminding you: you've made it to see another day. Each sip, bold and bitter, strong and smooth—just like us.

This book might be called *Espresso Yourself*, but for me, coffee has never just been about caffeine. It's been a metaphor, a ritual, a lifeline. A signal that no matter how exhausted, broken, or overwhelmed I felt, I still had something left in me. I could still rise. Even if it was with shaky hands and tear-filled eyes—I rose anyway.

I didn't always know I was resilient. And I sure as hell didn't always feel strong. I used to think strength meant having no cracks. Now I know resilience means surviving *with* the cracks—letting the light in through them.

Mornings I Didn't Want to Wake Up

I've had mornings when I sat on the edge of my bed, paralyzed—not because I was lazy, but because my soul was exhausted. I've had days where brushing my teeth felt like climbing a mountain. I would stare at my coffee mug, waiting for it to give me the energy I couldn't seem to find anywhere else.

There were days I prayed for silence but couldn't escape the noise in my own mind. Days when I was a mother, a wife, a CEO, a patient, a caregiver, a fighter... and I didn't know how to be *any* of those things anymore. My body was breaking down from illness. My mind was on the edge. My spirit felt like it was cracking.

But something inside me whispered:
Just make the coffee.

So I did. One shaky breath at a time. One sip. One step. That's how I moved forward.

That's how I survived.

Sometimes survival looks like crawling before you can walk again.

The Bitter Blend of Life

Resilience doesn't happen on the sunny days. It's brewed in the storms.

I know what it's like to be betrayed by people I loved. I know what it's like to feel invisible, like screaming in a crowded room but no one hears you. I know the ache of losing my sweet baby Mario—carrying him for almost nine months and then losing him in a way that shatters something inside of you that can never be put back quite the same.

I've had cancer show up like an uninvited guest—multiple times. I've battled autoimmune issues that left me exhausted and wondering how much more my body could take. I've watched people walk away when I needed them most. I've had to build from nothing more than grit, prayer, and hope... again and again.

But I'm still here. And that means something.

I've survived 100% of my worst days. And so have you.

That's not luck. That's resilience.

Espresso Yourself: The Moment I Stopped Apologizing

I spent years trying to make myself more "digestible." I tried to be the kind of woman people liked—smiling when I was hurting, staying silent when I should've spoken, dimming my light so others wouldn't feel uncomfortable.

But the truth is, I was never meant to be lukewarm. I'm not a bland, watery decaf. I'm a triple shot espresso, baby.

Bold. Unapologetic. Sometimes too much for people who prefer things light and sweet—but I'm not here to please the palette of the insecure.

I'm here to tell the truth. Even when it's messy.

I'm here to lead. Even when I'm scared.

I'm here to *live*. Even when I'm hurting.

I stopped apologizing for my voice. My fire. My scars. My ambition. My softness and my edge.

Because I've earned every ounce of who I am.

What Resilience Really Looks Like

Let's be honest—resilience is not glamorous.

It's not curated Instagram posts with clean filters and cute captions.

It's mascara-streaked cheeks in the school pickup line.

It's washing dishes while crying, then laughing five minutes later because your toddler said something hilarious and totally inappropriate.

It's sleeping in your car between doctor appointments and board meetings. It's still showing up to the meeting while battling nausea from chemo. It's holding your child while your heart breaks, but still making them dinner.

It's telling your team, "We got this," when you're not sure how you'll make payroll.

It's taking care of your family while your own body is screaming for rest.

Resilience is messy. But it's sacred.

And it's *so damn real.*

A Seat at the Table

There was a time when I thought I had to earn my place at the table by being polished and perfect.

Now? I *bring* the table.

I set the tone. I create the space. And I invite others in with their mess, their magic, their mid-breakdown moments, and their miracles.

I don't want surface-level conversations. I want the deep stuff.

Tell me how you made it through your worst year.
Tell me what keeps you up at night and what you're still dreaming of.
Tell me what you had to let go of in order to rise.
Tell me how you found the courage to love again.
Tell me what makes you laugh till you cry.

That's the table I want to sit at.

We don't need more highlight reels. We need more heart reels.

Resilience lives in the unfiltered, untamed, and unedited stories.

My Cup Runneth Over (Even When It's Empty)

There have been days when I've had nothing left to pour—but still poured anyway. That's what women do. We pour from empty cups, broken cups, chipped cups... and still make magic.

But over time, I've learned that pouring from an empty cup doesn't make me a hero. It makes me dehydrated—physically, emotionally, and spiritually.

So now, I brew differently.

I fill up first.

I sit in silence.

I pray. I cry. I write. I take walks. I dance. I breathe deep.

And I don't wait for permission anymore. My healing is my priority. My peace is not up for negotiation.

Pouring Into Others Without Losing Yourself

I've mentored, mothered, coached, and counseled women through some of the hardest times of their lives. And I've done it while going through hell myself.

Not because I'm superhuman. But because I *know* what it's like to feel like no one sees you.

I never want another woman to feel like she's alone in her pain.

That's why I created platforms, built businesses, wrote books, and launched movements—not for clout, but for connection. For community. For collaboration.

Because healing happens when we share our stories and pour our truth into one another's cups.

And sometimes, that starts with a simple question over coffee: *How are you—really?*

Brewing Joy Again

Grief taught me to cherish joy in small doses.

It's not always grand or glittery. Sometimes it's quiet and sacred.

Like my grandson's giggle.
A long hug from my daughter.
A dance in the kitchen.
A handwritten note.
A full night's sleep.
A moment of stillness.

Joy is not the absence of pain—it's the presence of love in the middle of it.

When I learned that, everything changed.

I didn't need life to be perfect to find joy. I just needed to pay attention.

My Daily Brew of Resilience

Here's my personal recipe for resilience—served hot, fresh, and honest:

- **1 shot of truth** – Own where you are. Name it. Don't sugarcoat it.
- **2 heaping spoons of grace** – You're allowed to mess up and still be amazing.
- **A dash of grit** – Remember what you've already survived. That's your evidence.
- **A sprinkle of joy** – Even when it's small. Especially when it's small.
- **A pour of faith** – You don't have to carry it all alone. Surrender the weight.

Stir gently. Sip slowly. Repeat daily.

Some days you'll forget a step. That's okay.

The point is—you showed up.

You brewed your cup.

And that, my friend, is everything.

From One Cup to Another

To the woman reading this who feels like she's drowning in expectations...

To the one who's holding it together for everyone else while falling apart inside...

To the one rebuilding her life, her business, her heart...

To the one rising from the ashes of betrayal, loss, or failure...

To the woman who's forgotten how powerful she is...

I see you.

You don't have to have it all figured out to be worthy.

You don't need to be perfect to be powerful.

You just have to be *you.*

Bold. Real. Resilient. And full of love.

Espresso yourself.

Fully.

Unapologetically.

And always remember—your story isn't over. Your cup isn't empty. You're just brewing the next chapter.

With all my heart,
Hanna

Debra Hornaday

Elementary Educator and Author

https://facebook.com/debbie.dee.75

Debbie Dee is author of Moments A Guided Gratitude Journal Designed to Reveal Your Happiness. She is a contributing author of Becoming Happy: 30 Ways to Heal Your Mind, Body and Soul. She always knew she wanted to help people. Debbie Dee began working in elementary education. She claims it is one of the best opportunities she has been afforded in life. There may be a lot of gloomy moments on her job, but she is grateful to help bring positivity to her students. Debbie Dee lives a life of gratitude. She is thankful for the blessings in her life. At any moment of the day, she will not hesitate to take time to be grateful for something in her life. She believes people can change their mindset in an instant just by focusing on something positive no matter how insignificant it may seem.

From Quiet Sips to Bold Brews: My Journey Through College and Beyond

By Debra Hornaday

When I think of espresso, I think of my coffee stories, experiences I have had with coffee. Doesn't everyone have a history with coffee, even if they are not a regular coffee drinker? I will be sharing my coffee stories with you in this excerpt.

I like the subtitle of this book, "A Cup of Resilience." I thought about all the life stories I would share here. I have had plenty of opportunity to display strength and to be resilient. Reflecting on my life, I decided I would share several facets of my college life. I begin with what happened at the outset of my four years while living on campus.

I will share some details about my work while being a full-time student and how it all panned out. As a young girl navigating her way through life while in college, I managed to accomplish my goals. Then, I was on to my next thing.

As a full-time college student, I had many experiences. It was all new to me. It was the first time I was away from my mom at length, except when my grandma used to babysit me.

College is the place where I grew up. I entered as a teenager. I left as a young adult. There were times when it was tough. But I also had fun. I met a lot of people, and I worked a lot.

I have plenty of stories about working various jobs while getting my degree. That is not unique. Most everyone has a job while they are in school. I have not taken a poll or anything like that. But that is what I presume. So, let's get to it!

I got hired for a job before classes even started. I had been assigned to a work-study job. That is when a student is awarded a job on campus because of a financial need. It was part of my financial aid package.

Whoo hoo! How exciting was that? I had spending money while living on campus. It certainly was a blessing to me.

When I received my paycheck, I could take some of it to the financial aid office to help pay my tuition. The rest I could keep for fun and expenses.

I didn't have to travel far to work. It was a five-minute walk from my dorm room. My campus was small. This made things convenient for me.

But at one point, I thought I needed more money. So, I got a job off campus. I attended the same college all four years while earning my bachelor's degree. Therefore, I had a few off-campus jobs as well.

Here's where the fun began. I was juggling a full-time schedule of classes, working on campus, and working off campus.

In addition, I decided to get involved in extracurricular activities. This was important to me because I felt I needed opportunities to practice my communication skills.

Participating in various organizations and clubs would help eliminate my shyness. As a matter of fact, I am a self-proclaimed introvert. Growing up, I was a quiet person more than anything. Still, I did not want to be like that. I wanted to be a more vocal personality.

As a young girl, I was the quiet one at home and at school. But this teenager wanted to be more outgoing. Upon entering college, I had a conversation with myself. I told myself that I was going to come out of my shell. Eventually, I accomplished my goal.

This is a nice segue about the first job I want to share. Prior to going away to college, I worked at a fabric store. So, when I went away to college, I applied with the same company and I got hired.

Working for this employer was fun, but it was a chore getting to work. I had to walk to the bus stop. Then, I would take the city bus to another part of town.

Fortunately, my boss allowed me to work daytime hours. I never had to ride the bus home in the dark. That was a good thing.

Here is something special that happened while I was working at the fabric store. One day, my boss asked me if I wanted to be a sewing machine salesperson. Say what? Who me? It was one of those, "Who are you talking to, Willis?" moments.

I thought long and hard for a day or two about why she would ask me to take that assignment. I tried picturing myself selling sewing machines. All I could think was, I would not know what to say to customers, and I would be bored.

Because of my limited thinking, I would not be successful as a sewing machine salesperson. I hated to have to tell my boss, "Thanks but no thanks." Eventually, I did. She smiled and said, "OK."

Here is the reason she asked me to take that assignment. She told me that I was a good talker. Who was a good talker? I was a good talker.

I had already begun my transformation into becoming a social butterfly. Maybe not. But I was accomplishing my goal by becoming a better communicator.

Fast-forward to the present, I have a career that requires me to talk a lot. I am grateful for the many opportunities I have been afforded in my current assignment. If I tell someone that I used to be very quiet and shy, they don't believe me. Let's just say that we evolve. I did.

I am a person who has tried many things. But a lot of my earlier jobs were rooted in retail. One day, I heard a major retailer was coming to town, where I attended college. They needed people to "open" the store.

I was up for the task. I interviewed for a position, and I got hired. All of us new hires were responsible for stocking shelves, organizing merchandise, and getting the store ready for business. It was a good experience.

I ended up working in one of the departments selling carpets and drapes. I thought this would be the most boring assignment ever.

I didn't think I was cut out to sell carpets, but I learned a lot. Although boring at times, it was a good situation for me.

I met a customer who understood the trials and ordeals of a college student. We struck up a conversation, and I told him about my studio apartment I had just moved into.

He and his wife came to my apartment. They gave me their extra twin-size bed. It was perfect for the little studio I lived in. It was the cutest little apartment right across the street from my college campus.

Also, that man was responsible for me getting hired in a science laboratory at the university across town. I don't know why I got hired. I think a higher power was looking out for me. I was assigned a unique task.

I couldn't describe the insects I transported from one container to another if you paid me. I didn't know the names of these insects nor the purpose of this entire operation. For me, it was a job to help get me through college. It served its purpose, and for that, I am grateful.

Let me sidestep for a moment. This book you are reading is all about encouraging women to reclaim their power. As you read my story, you will see how I was "doing college," starting out as a teenager. The four years I spent on that college campus would be the foundation for my future career and my adult life. I don't know if I was reclaiming any power. But I was learning to use my power and to get things done.

Hopefully, something you'll glean from my story will be beneficial to you, the reader. As you learn about the women in this book, you will begin to craft your own story.

* * *

What about the academic part of my college life? I can say I didn't know what to expect. However, I thought it would be fun and very easy. After all, I had chosen to study fashion. How hard could that be?

I was excited as I signed up to study fashion merchandising. But when I found out I would have to take an accounting class, a couple of math classes, business classes, history classes, and other similar classes, I was disappointed. What happened to all the fun classes where you talk about fashion? Of course, I had to take those as well.

I had learned to sew as a young girl. Also, I had experience in retail prior to going away to college. Therefore, I figured studying fashion merchandising would be a breeze.

As I am describing my college experience, I hope you will see it as my testimony. But I hope you see yourself doing the same. See yourself as a doer, a person who progresses and does what is needed to accomplish your goal. Be or become a "lifelong learner."

I had heard of the phrase "lifelong learner" from time to time when I was younger. I did not fully grasp the meaning of it. However, as a mature adult, I have learned what it means. I am a person who is interested in many things. I try many things. You can, too.

My four-year college experience included a variety of experiences, including becoming a member of a sorority. It was an amazing experience that took a lot of time away from my academic studies.

As I was going through the process to join the organization, I had a full load of classes and a job. I nearly flunked out of my classes during that semester. There was too much happening at once.

I managed to salvage some of my grades. I only earned six credits during this particular semester. But I made up for it by attending summer school. Also, I took more than a basic load of classes the following semester.

I was determined to graduate on time. It cost too much to attend that small private institution. Also, I didn't want to attend college longer than necessary.

If I could graduate in four years, why would I stay longer? I ended up being on track to graduate in 3 1/2 years. But I wasn't prepared to enter the "real world." I stayed the course and graduated after four years of diligence and hard work.

Up to now, I have given you a snapshot of my college experience. There are so many encouraging and not-so-sweet moments to share.

I could talk about the time I went to court to testify on behalf of my neighbors. They were fighting with another neighbor. I found myself right in the middle of it all.

How about the time I signed up to take voice lessons? I attended the first session, and I learned how to dog pant. I left the music office and went straight to the administration office to "drop" that class.

I didn't sign up to do calisthenics with my abdomen while breathing rapidly through my mouth. Something just wasn't right. Your girl here didn't have a clue about the instrument called the voice and the preparation it took to develop it.

Around my second or third year in college was the time I started my health journey, while attempting to be a vegetarian. I almost passed out a couple of times walking across campus because of a nutrient deficiency. It was serious.

I went to the doctor, and he stuck me with a needle. Dang! He pumped some ferrous sulfate into me. Ah, don't worry. It's a fancy name for iron. I just needed an occasional burger, I suppose.

Then there's the time some guy wrote a song for me. He played it and sang it to me.

It was the sweetest gesture. But I wasn't feeling him or that song. I probably only saw him one more time ever. Bye, boy. He was gone!

How about the time someone gave me a vehicle? It was a Chevy. That thing sat in the driveway for months before I gave it away. I didn't have a driver's license, and I didn't have much experience driving. I didn't know anyone to help me figure it out.

The reason why I am sharing my story is that sharing stories is a good way to get your point across. Also, people are usually interested in other people's stories. Well, I am. Plus it is a great way to make connections, and to learn from one another.

I was researching Stanford's LEAD online class program. A class is offered where you can learn about the power of story. I read, "Studies show that we are wired to remember stories much more than data, facts, and figures." Also, about stories, "They paint a picture of what could be for everyone."

That is why I am sharing so much about my experience. It's my story. You, the reader, can begin reflecting on your life experiences. Maybe you want to do your own storytelling one day.

If you're reluctant to write or if you don't feel like you do not write well enough, start by journaling. Write to yourself and for yourself. Who knows, maybe you will do some blogging, participate in an anthology, or write your own book.

You could take it to the stage like I plan to do one day. Maybe you have a dream that never materialized. Listen up, seniors. I heard that it is not too late, even if you are up there in age.

Have you heard of Grandma Moses? She taught herself how to paint. But she didn't start painting until she was in her seventies.

Someone said if she had begun painting at an early age like Picasso, she would have been on the same level as him. Even though her paintings didn't make millions, she did receive $100,000 at some point for her work. Hey, let's meet at the art store this weekend. We have some painting to do.

I am grateful for my college experience. I shared just a snapshot of what happened. I suppose I will lay out more details when another opportunity is presented.

Being grateful has become a part of my daily routine. Andrew Huberman from Stanford says, the most effective gratitude practice is "receiving gratitude or observing someone else receiving gratitude." I won't spend time with all that data talk.

But I give gratitude, and I receive it. I feel this practice has been instrumental in my life. Hopefully, you will learn to benefit from the practice of gratitude as well. I declare it is life-changing for me.

I am grateful for my many opportunities during my college years and in life. How it worked out for me to attend that small private institution was beyond me at the time.

See, my family did not have money to send me to school. That is one of the reasons I always worked a job or two at the same time. I felt like it was a necessary part of my journey.

In the end, I obtained a bachelor's degree in fashion merchandising. I learned all the layers of the industry, from business to the pattern-making and design side.

I already knew how to sew from a "store-bought" pattern. But in my program, I learned how to make a pattern from scratch. It was difficult, but I was able to create wonderful, finished garments in the end.

I studied window display and learned how to attract customers into the store. I learned about modeling and participated in fashion shows presented by the Fashion Department. I had a wonderful experience, and for that, I am grateful.

What do I want you to get out of this chapter? I want you to be inspired by that teenage girl who had a dream; one who experienced life and accomplished her goals. I want you to do it as well.

There is no need to be reluctant or afraid. Figure out what you want and get to work. If it appears to be too big a task, break it down into smaller chunks.

Haven't you heard, "Rome wasn't built in a day"? Don't you know how to eat an elephant? One bite at a time, of course. You got this. You can do it.

I have been in my current career for several years. It is the career I will retire from. But I dream about what could happen next. I still have goals.

My most recent goal was to publish my first solo book. I accomplished that goal on December 20, 2023. It has been an amazing learning experience.

Being an author has opened opportunities to meet other authors. That is how I learned about SHE RISES STUDIOS. This platform makes it possible for me and you to bring our dreams to fruition.

Set goals, learn from others, and make things happen. I'm here for you as well. If you want to know more about my story, check out my book. It is *Moments A Guided Gratitude Journal Designed to Reveal Your Happiness*. To make it simple, type Moments Journal by Debbie Dee. It will pop up on your device.

In conclusion, I promised to tell you my coffee stories. I will share one here.

When I was five or six years old, I used to see my grandma drink coffee. I asked her what it does for her.

I thought she said, "It helps me calm down so I could go to sleep." Hum. I decided to "calm down" one night when it was my bedtime.

You probably know what happened. My little body was wired, and I did not calm down.

As an adult, I was never a coffee drinker. I didn't even know how to make coffee.

Finally, I learned how to make it, and it tastes great! I am the staff barista where I work, and for that, my coworkers are grateful. Hopefully, you learned something from my chapter, and by the way, I receive the gratitude!

Jen Rigley

Founder of Flourishing Over Fifty

https://www.linkedin.com/in/jenrigley/
https://www.facebook.com/flourishingoverfifty
https://www.instagram.com/flourishingoverfifty/
https://flourishingoverfifty.com/

Jen Rigley is an author, motivational speaker and personal transformation expert focused on women's empowerment and living your best life after 50. Her mission is to inspire and empower women in midlife to create a new story for their life, especially after facing significant challenges and trauma. Formerly a top sales and marketing executive working with both start-ups and Fortune 500 clients, Jen is the founder of Flourishing Over Fifty, a brand whose powerful message is rooted in overcoming adversity in midlife. With years of real-life experience encountering and overcoming significant trauma and challenges Jen is sought after to share her story of resilience and triumphing over adversity. As a well-respected leader in women's empowerment, Jen inspires thousands of women to overcome challenges, heal and flourish in midlife through her Flourishing Over Fifty community and her Flourish Journey Framework.

The Gift of Resilience: From Loss to Light - Create a New Story for Your Life

By Jen Rigley

Can you envision your perfect day? Close your eyes and take a few minutes to begin dreaming about how your perfect day unfolds. Allow yourself to be fully present, connecting deeply to each of your senses, and feel what resonates with you.

- SIGHT: What does your perfect day look like? Do you see yourself at the beach, in your cozy home, on a mountain top, or surrounded by your loved ones?

- TOUCH: What does your perfect day feel like? Can you feel the hot sand on your feet, that perfect soft blanket on your legs, the breeze as you approach the top of the mountain, or those special hugs from your kids?

- SOUND: What does your perfect day sound like? Can you hear the soothing rhythm of waves slowly rolling on the shore, your favorite melody playing softly, the quietness atop a mountain, or the joyful laughter of family?

- TASTE: What does your perfect day taste like? Do you feel the icy coolness of a popsicle, the savory flavor of your special homemade bread, the smooth, sweet richness of a peanut butter and jelly sandwich eaten after reaching the peak, or the crunch of a bowl of popcorn shared with all?

- SMELL: What aromas surround you on this perfect day? Can you breathe in that special mix of sand and sea, the scent of your favorite candle, the pine needles from the towering trees along your hike, or the many scents made up of each of your children?

How beautiful it is that we can summon all of our senses to envision our perfect life?

While envisioning our perfect day helps us understand what we want in our lives, the truth is that many of us wake up every day, stepping not into our perfect lives, but with the weight of our lives pressing upon us. It feels like we are carrying a weighted blanket on our shoulders, with a heaviness that slows our steps and saps our energy. It is usually not one event that is weighing on us, but rather a lifetime of accumulated grief, trauma, loss, and challenges, built up, layer after layer, year after year. Resilience is what allows us to keep going. As we face each loss, each challenge, we build up our resilience. It is what keeps us marching in the forward direction. Some of us have quite the stockpile of resilience, and that is why it is not surprising that we can find ourselves mired in deep despair.

When we experience repeated loss, when we've built up our stockpile of resilience, it only holds us up for so long. There comes a day when we aren't able to enjoy life fully or create that perfect day. Sometimes, it is years of loss, trauma, and challenges that we have endured and powered through that have worn us down and faded the joy in our lives.

Research confirms that loss, unresolved emotional pain, and the cumulative weight of life's difficulties impact our mental, emotional, and even physical well-being, altering the way we show up in our relationships, careers, and daily lives.[1] And while resilience keeps us going, the effects may ripple through every aspect of our being, and that is how we come to be carrying a weighted blanket on our shoulders.

The cumulative weight of loss, grief, and challenges affects each one of us in a different way—we each have our own unique blanket to carry. For some of us, this weight manifests as the struggle to get out of bed in the morning. Others of us manage to go boldly about our day, carrying that despair deep inside. We show up as best we can for our family, for our friends, for our job.

I know this feeling intimately because I lived it for a long time. The challenge is that, eventually, this catches up to us—our resilience starts to run low. The busyness that goes on beneath that weighted blanket can only hide despair for so long.

For me, it caught up to me when I found myself lying flat out on the kitchen floor, tears streaming down my face, my body pressed against the cool tiles. The grief of losing my mother had cracked open a vault of past sorrow, and suppressed memories surfaced like a tidal wave. My resilience had run out, my stockpile was empty. My mind replayed the mantra, "Is this all there is?"—a question that haunted me after years of working hard, overcoming traumatic experiences, and striving to create a meaningful life. At that moment, I struggled to see any point in continuing the fight. I did not know how I was going to pick myself up and get back to living, get back to caring for my children, and get back to my job.

As I lay there on the kitchen floor, truly grief-stricken for my mother's passing, all my past grief started bubbling up. Memories and feelings that I had suppressed for so long were floating through my mind. A ticker tape that said, "Is this all there is to life?" was running round and round. After working so hard to build a good life, to be a good person, to raise my daughters in a meaningful manner, to quickly overcome multiple traumatic experiences (thank you resilience)... all I could think was, "Is this all there is?" Life just didn't seem worth the struggle any longer. I lived in this space and walked through life for a long time with this running in my head. If you had asked me my story, it would have started and ended with a list of challenges and losses. None of the good stuff—my focus was always on all the things that had gone wrong, the people I had lost, the challenges that I had. There was no more resilience to be found.

I first faced loss when I was a little girl. My father had been in the hospital and was home, spending his days on our beloved blue velvet couch while he recovered. One night I had a dream, a terrible dream. A dream no little girl wants to have. In my dream, I heard something bumping the walls in our hallway, right outside my bedroom door. In my dream, I saw a stretcher being pushed down the hallway by men in white coats. I could hear the murmur of voices. In my dream, I had the vision that my father was being taken out of the house on a stretcher.

I woke up the morning after this terrible dream, just like it was any other day. A day for me to go to school, a day for me to play with my friends. But when I walked downstairs, I was a bit confused because everyone turned to look at me, and there were people in my house who wouldn't typically be there on a regular morning. It was then that I knew my dream had not been a dream at all. Suddenly, I knew that at age 10, my life, my family's life, would never be the same and that my father would never be coming home. My mother was left to raise six children on her own.

My father's tragic death when he was just 42 years old was just one of several losses I have endured. It started my pattern of storing my grief deep inside, hiding it from myself and the world. As life went on, I endured several other tragedies. One year, my brother-in-law was killed by a drunk driver on Thanksgiving. I stored that grief deep down. The following year, my sister died in a car accident. I stored that grief deep down. It was like a layer cake, one grief being layered on top of another while resilience took charge and helped me move forward.

That day when I found myself lying on the kitchen floor after the loss of my mother came at a time in my life when I was faced with another series of challenges that came one after another. I lost my job and was diagnosed with breast cancer. I fought to keep that grief buried deep, but I could no longer. I know that you, too, have been in situations where the losses and challenges keep coming, maybe more than you think you can handle.

It was while lying there on the kitchen floor, ruminating over what had become my mantra, "Is this all there is to life?" when I heard a whisper, which I believe was from my mother, my father, and my sister. The message was clear: "Yes, life is hard, and you have had your share of loss. But your family, your friends, and your daughters need you. There is work to be done, but you can, you will, begin to enjoy life. You will find joy again."

That moment became the turning point in my healing. I realized I didn't have to remain defined by grief—I had the power to create a new story for my life, to reclaim my joy, and to help others do the same. And so began my journey of renewal.

Today, I know deeply that even after profound loss and trauma, resilience is possible. Healing is possible. Joy is absolutely possible.

My own healing journey led me to create **The Flourish Journey™**, a transformative seven-step framework designed specifically to help women like you reclaim the life you deserve.

The healing process is a complex journey, but there are two key activities that are part of The Flourish Journey™ framework that you can follow to truly begin the healing process. Both of these were instrumental to my healing process. These can help you create a new story for your life, and to craft a life you love—one that is authentic, fulfilling, and inspiring.

The foundational step is a simple yet powerful daily practice - The Quiet Reclaiming with The Joy Triangle©. Stillness clears the mind, gratitude softens the heart, and intention directs the soul.

Foundation

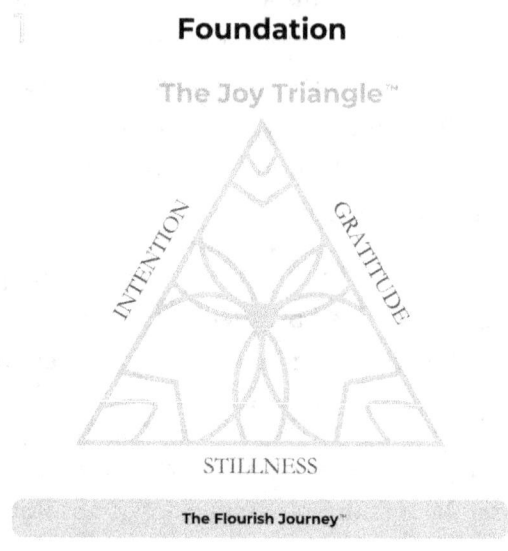

The Joy Triangle™

INTENTION

GRATITUDE

STILLNESS

The Flourish Journey™

1. Stillness – 1 minute: Sit in silence, allowing yourself to quiet your mind.
2. Gratitude – 1 minute: Reflect on what you are grateful for.
3. Intention – 1 minute: Set a meaningful intention for your day.

By dedicating just three minutes to this daily practice, you will begin to shift your perspective, move beyond despair, and start thinking about the joy to come in your life, setting the foundation for lasting transformation. Over time, these small moments create a ripple effect, altering the trajectory of your life.

Another step within The Flourish Journey™ is to understand at a deep level what your life is today, so you have clarity around what is good and what needs to be changed. This is The Flourish Checkpoint: Current Life Assessment. You can't move forward in an intentional, meaningful way until you are clear about what today feels like—you can't change tomorrow if you don't understand today. The best way to do this is to perform a life assessment. After a lot of reflection, I began to assess every area of my life, focusing on five key questions:

- What and who do you like?
- What and who do you love?
- What and who is hurting you?
- What and who is missing from your life?
- What and who is holding you back?

By answering these honestly, you'll gain profound clarity, empowering yourself to nurture what uplifts you and lovingly release what no longer serves you.

By gaining clarity on these aspects, you can make conscious decisions to nurture what uplifts you and release what no longer serves you. By truly understanding the answers to these questions, you can make meaningful, authentic, and lasting changes in your life.

If it doesn't lift you, love you, or lead you forward—let it go. The objective over time is to nurture the people, things, and activities that lift you up and to release the people, things, and activities that weigh you down. You, and only you, get to decide what you want to keep and what you need to eliminate to move toward your ideal tomorrow.

The Flourish Journey™ and creating a new story for your life is about reclaiming your power, your voice, and ultimately, your joy.

I want you to know that your pain does not define you. You are resilient beyond measure, worthy of love, happiness, and deep fulfillment. Your past doesn't have to dictate your future.

I see you, I honor your journey, and I genuinely believe in the joy-filled life that awaits you.

You don't have to stay stuck or keep your despair hidden. Right now, gently lift yourself from wherever you are—even if metaphorically still on the kitchen floor—and take that first loving step toward healing.

Once you have completed these two steps, it is time to perform the perfect day visioning activity again. Can you envision your perfect day? Close your eyes and take a few minutes to begin dreaming about how your perfect day unfolds. Allow yourself to be fully present, connecting deeply to each of your senses, and feel what resonates with you.

Create a new story for your life. Join the Flourishing Over Fifty® community and reclaim your joy, rewrite your story, and flourish—together.

Scan the QR code or follow the link to join the Flourishing Over Fifty community, receive a free gift, and take your first step towards the life you truly deserve.

SCAN ME

https://bit.ly/hannaselfcare

Follow on Social Media to get your daily dose of inspiration:

https://www.facebook.com/flourishingoverfifty
https://www.instagram.com/flourishingoverfifty/
https://flourishingoverfifty.com/subscribe-page/

[1] https://www.ncbi.nlm.nih.gov/books/NBK207191/#top

Suzanne E Minshew

Founder of Zannie Goods

https://www.facebook.com/share/193xes6LiR/
https://www.instagram.com/zannie_minshew/

Suzanne is a wife, mom of 3 and grandma to 2, and loves the Lord and her family beyond measure. She has a BA from Hiram College and has had a successful career in management, recruiting and career coaching as well as Healthcare with smatterings of volunteer work focused primarily on fundraising. Throughout her career she has been afforded the opportunity to do extensive amounts of writing from standard orders of procedures and company policies to employee hero stories and media releases. She has rekindled a love of writing and is developing a portfolio of poetry and short stories, which she will hopefully share with the world one day. Her biggest passion is healing and helping those along their own journey of healing. After a tumultuous upbringing and many mistakes along the way, she has focused her adult life on trusting the Lord and finding healing for herself, mentally, physically, emotionally and spiritually. Her prayer is that you find some nugget of healing or inspiration within her writings to find healing for yourself.

Speak Love

By Suzanne E Minshew

Our lives could begin as a story of hardship and pain or with roses and butterflies, but how we live our lives and experience each moment is a testimony of where it all begins in our minds. How we think about ourselves, our experiences, the people and the world around us, it all begins with one little thought, and how we react to and perceive ourselves in those moments is pivotal in how our lives will go. Are we victims or are we victors? Welcome to my journey of the war of voices in my mind. How it began, how I have overcome and persevered, and how I live a victorious life today.

My story begins with my first thought of myself. As nearly as I can remember, I felt like an afterthought, a burden, someone who had no significance in the world. Expectations were clear: I was to respect my elders. Do not speak unless spoken to, clean your plate, and give the house a good name, but never ask for seconds because then you'll get "big and fat like Tom and Jean," whoever they were. I was a victim of my circumstances, a divorced mom who took my brother and me across the country to settle near family with whom I bounced around, and finally lived with my grandparents for several years before my mother felt able to care for me while working as an elementary school teacher. The words and innuendos spoken over me from the time I was little was "she talks to much, she is a burden, she eats too much, she doesn't clean her plate, she has so much potential, she is like her father (which wasn't a good thing), she is so messy, she is talented, but, she is so smart, but, she doesn't measure up, she spends money too quickly, she is not worthy, she could be, blah, blah blah, if only she would blah, blah, blah." I was ignored. I became a performer on the stage of life, gaining attention when I performed well and when I didn't. I got lots of praise and attention when I performed in a show or sang a song or did a recital. Behind the scenes, I was ignored, criticized, or simply alone. Expectations were high, but there was no guidance, no teaching, only shame, rigid rules, and condemnation. I went to six different schools in elementary school, so I had few friends and felt insignificant in my academic world. Middle school and high school were a bit different, though I couldn't make up for my social deficits, so I became a chameleon. I adapted to my environment and never really allowed myself to form opinions, establish what I liked or disliked, beyond the most blatant to my senses. I set myself up to be the victim more often than I can count, mostly with boys, but as my peers grew around me and found their voices, I remained incapable. I was trapped inside a body filled with pain and anger, frustration and fear, unworthiness and, worst of all, shame.

There was no specific day or time when a switch was flipped and I ran through the fields of Austria singing songs of freedom, speaking nothing but love and life to myself. It has been a lifetime of healing. College did not bring healing or a change in the words that I spoke to myself. I adapted like the good chameleon I was, but I never quite fit in, so I was constantly changing friend groups, burning bridges, self-sabotaging, all the unhealthy things people do when they feel unworthy of love. It was at this point that I began a path of self-destruction that had culminated from years of true self-loathing. This was a five-year period of darkness for me. I hated myself. Hated the way I looked, the way I talked, the way I could never measure up to anyone else. I felt stupid and incapable of doing anything. I drank too much. I starved myself. I overate. I became a loner and exhibited risky behaviors, involving myself with those who loved me less than I loved myself, if that is possible. I was depressed all the time, never spoke a kind word to myself, and prayed that I would go to sleep and never wake up. It is amazing to me that I survived, but I did. By God's good grace, I did.

From this rock bottom, I had nowhere to go but upwards, so I surrendered myself to the Lord and took every opportunity that presented itself to change my life. I was sick and tired of being sick and tired. I immersed myself in 12-step programs (it didn't matter to me what the "drug of choice" was; the principles were all the same) and therapy multiple times a week. I read my Bible every day and began to pray away the darkness of my heart. My sponsor and my therapist became the human voices in my head, speaking truth and love and life into my broken soul. I can still see my therapist, Janet Faye, with her hippie vibe, leaning over a canvas telling me what a beautiful heart I had for other people and that it was time to share that with myself. I can hear my first sponsor, sharing with me that I was not crazy, that being a child of an alcoholic, the words spoken over me during my upbringing were not accurate, were not from a place of love, and were not normal. She conveyed that God loved me, just as I am. That I am worthy of love. I am worthy of goodness in my life. That I am worthy of so much more than I had received. That God wept when I felt shamed or blamed or unloved. These were the beautiful words that were showered on me for over a year, DAILY. And you know what? I began to believe.

Since those early days, I have spent the last 30-plus years exercising the "three steps forward, one or two steps back" philosophy. Not intentionally, of course, but it seems to ring true. At different times in my healing process, I have sought out therapy, working on different issues, gleaning what I need in those times to get unstuck. It has helped me gain a new perspective, make adjustments as needed, and continue to move forward.

I have spent lots and lots of time with myself, in discovery. What do I like? What don't I like? Who am I? Where does my significance lie? Here are some of my discoveries. I love the Lord and love learning more about Him. I owe Him my life. I love to laugh! After trying all the flavors at Baskin-Robbins, I have several favorites, and they depend on the season of the year and the general mood of the day. My summertime favorite is strawberry. When I am feeling nostalgic,

I default to Butter Pecan because it reminds me of the sweet days of being with my grandparents. I definitely don't like anything that includes black licorice, nor will I ever, in this lifetime, like liver. My favorite color is teal, blue, not green. I love big soft sweaters and sweatshirts, but also love a nice fitting women's t-shirt or dress that molds to the curves of the womanly body God gave me. I love the sun, warm weather, and sweet summer rain. I love gardening. I love music of all kinds, but remain selective based on how it moves my soul. I love classic cars, riding motorcycles, writing, history, hiking, nature, and singing. I love people who are encouraging and kind and loving and transparent. And so much more. There is so much to love about this life!

I don't like clothing that is scratchy or poky; music that makes my ears hurt or my senses pained. I don't like people who take advantage of others or are unkind; I do not like snow that lasts forever or icy road conditions. I definitely don't like to be lazy or disconnected. More here, too.

Who am I? I am the daughter of the King Most High, who is loved and forgiven. I am human and I make mistakes, but through the blood of Jesus, I am redeemed. I am not perfect, but I am honest and will own up to my mistakes. I am a wife, a mother, a grandmother, a sister, a niece, an aunt, a friend, a mentor, and so on. All roles that I take seriously, that I have learned much from, and still work to grow in. I am beautiful, loving, kind, and creative. I am an advocate, a protector, a warrior, and so much more.

My significance lies in one thing only, and that is Jesus Christ. For when I keep my eyes on Him, I am following His path for me.

All of these self-discoveries have been from experiments, exercises, and life experiences. Through books I have read, music or podcasts I have listened to, or simply those who are in my life or have been encountered along my life's path. Always asking myself, "Do I

REALLY like it?" In the beginning, it was very basic. I enveloped the process of developing my opinions on things that many have already decided upon. Favorite color, food, song, book, movie, clothing, weather, etc. Then I moved on to people. What are the characteristics of a good friend or partner? What about a husband? How does this person make me feel when I am with them, and how do I feel when they leave? Then I graduated to how I affect people and what my motivations are when in a relationship. How do I make people feel, and how do they feel when I leave? Growing, growing, growing!

One of the most significant books I read in that early period of healing was *Codependency No More* by Melody Beatty. Through her words, I discovered that setting boundaries is healthy. That I needn't be a doormat for every person that comes along, nor do I have to save everyone. I can love myself enough to live my life and be a healthy support to those who truly love and care about me. What a gift this book was to me then, and now, in review, perhaps I need to read it again. Her words were like having a spotlight shine down on me and show me that I don't need to live in the shadows of the world, but I can live front and center, living a healthy life, speaking all the good things that each of us needs to hear. You are worthy. You are loving. You are blessed. You are God's beautiful gift to the world. Shine and be what He made you to be!

I have used tools like self-affirmations on my bathroom mirror, in my car, on my phone, on my desk at work, anywhere and everywhere. In the beginning, I desperately needed to be showered in love and self-love, affirmation, and self-affirmation, retraining my brain and my general attitude towards myself to be kind and loving, replacing all of the negatives instilled from childhood. Sometimes, I still need it. Life can be unkind. I am human and those around me are just as human, so mistakes are made, feelings are hurt, and consequences are suffered. Asking for forgiveness, forgiving myself (not an easy thing, especially when I've hurt someone I truly love), and making things right have been key for me, but allowing myself to stop the negative thoughts and revisit affirmations of God's love and my own love for myself has been invaluable. I made a mistake. I asked for forgiveness, I made it right, and all I can do now is to forgive myself and move on. I can be proud of my efforts and love myself for trying.

Beyond those tools of affirmation, I listen to people like Joyce Meyer, Lisa Terkhurst, Kaye Warren, Jack Hibbs, Gary Hemrick, Billy Graham, Chuck Smith, Priscilla Shirer, Christine Caine, and more who all have provided me healing of different parts of me through their teachings. Each has their own story of healing and/or biblical teaching that has provided me comfort, understanding, and gentle guidance as I traverse this beautiful life I get to live. I attend a Bible study that has provided me with a solid group of women who love me and pray for me, shoring me up against the battles of darkness that continue to wage war against me and those I love. They provide beauty and truth, sparkles and giggles, and a great big dose of laughter, often!

Where I once wavered in faith and my walk with the Lord, today it is nearly untouchable. God and I have weathered storms of physical, mental abuse, and domestic violence to a point of victory. He carried me when I thought I would lose our second child in utero. He offered confidence, creativity, and security as my husband engaged in full-time graduate school while I had a more than full-time job and three kids at home. He provided friends along the way who helped to shuffle kids to activities and provide support. He was in all of the details of my worrying and grieving over our children at different times during their upbringing. God was there when making difficult decisions that may or may not have been the right ones. God held me close when our middle son chose to take his life at age 20. He still holds me close as I continue to pray for our oldest, who has a big job, a wife, and two small children, and our youngest, who is in an abusive relationship. God also rejoices in the strides that I have made over the years. He rejoices in how I tend to my grief that lingers and how I still speak affirming words to myself.

Today I have grown to the point of not only speaking affirmations of love and kindness to myself, but over others as well. I write poetry of God's love for gifts to those whom I treasure. I speak love and kindness to those I meet, and I write my stories of survival, of delivery, of healing, and now of self-love in hopes that just one person is helped along their path of healing.

So, let me ask you. What are you saying to yourself today? Are you vilifying yourself over a mistake you made, or have you found a way to forgive yourself? Are you making excuses or are you trying to learn from your mistakes, make changes, and move forward? Are you being loving and kind to yourself? Have you worked to heal the pains of your past? Are you treating yourself as well or better than other relationships in your life? I pray that you are.

We are all a work in progress, so as long as there is breath, there is no ending to our healing. No ending to our relationship with ourselves. No end to finding new and creative ways in which to love and honor ourselves. May we all love, honor, and respect ourselves so much that we treat our beautiful selves as the true royalty that we are. Exquisite, magnificent, honorable, worthy daughters of the King Most High!

Helen Holden Slottje

Founder of Regenerative Law Institute
Dimensional Alchemist

https://www.linkedin.com/in/helenslottje/
https://www.instagram.com/hslottje/?hl=en
https://www.instagram.com/hslottje/?hl=en
www.regenerativelaw.com

Helen Holden Slottje embodies the art of transformative resilience. A Harvard-educated attorney and Goldman Environmental Prize recipient, she pioneered legal strategies that achieved the once-impossible statewide ban on fracking in New York. Where others saw only binary choices—adapt to extraction or protest its inevitability—Helen perceived dimensional possibilities invisible to conventional thinking. Through what she terms Stereographic Intelligencesm, Helen repurposed zoning ordinances into tools for community sovereignty, transforming not just what communities did but what governance itself could be. Her approach transcended mere resistance or adaptation, making the inevitable impossible, and the impossible inevitable. Helen's work exemplifies how disruption becomes not merely a challenge to endure but a threshold to cross—a dimensional gateway to possibilities beyond current imagination. As founder of the regenerative law institute, she helps others navigate beyond the endless trap of resilience-as-endurance into truly transformative capacity, evolving greater harmony and possibility.

Beyond Bouncing Back: Stereographic Intelligence℠

By Helen Holden Slottje

The Paradox of Resilience

Resilience has become a celebrated virtue in our culture—the capacity to recover from setbacks, adapt to change, and persevere through hardship. We admire the resilient individual, community, or ecosystem that withstands pressure and returns to form. Yet within this seemingly straightforward concept lies a profound paradox that has remained largely unexamined.

What if our conventional understanding of resilience—the ability to "bounce back" from adversity—actually functions as a sophisticated trap? What if the very quality we celebrate for its strength simultaneously functions as a mechanism that maintains systems of domination rather than transforming them?

What happens when we consider resilience not merely as a quality of endurance but as a dimensional capacity—one that can either confine us to cycles of adaptation without transformation or liberate us into new possibilities beyond current limitation? When we examine resilience through the lens of dimensional intelligence, we discover how this essential capacity might be reclaimed from its co-optation by systems that value endurance over liberation.

The Lemniscate Trap: Resilience as Eternal Return

Consider the infinity, figure-eight symbol, mathematically known as a lemniscate (∞). In two dimensions, it appears to cross over itself, creating a point of intersection where paths converge and diverge. This geometric form offers a powerful metaphor for understanding how resilience functions within what Audre Lorde short-handed as the **Master's House**—structures of domination, extraction, and control that shape our social, economic, and ecological realities.

From a two-dimensional perspective, resilience appears as continuous movement along this figure-eight path. We encounter challenges at the crossing point—moments of crisis, disruption, or trauma—and then navigate beyond them, only to eventually return to similar challenges in an endless loop. The resilient person or community becomes adept at navigating these crossing points, developing increasingly sophisticated strategies for recovery.

Yet herein lies the trap: what appears as virtuous adaptation often functions as circular containment. We become skilled at enduring recurring crises without ever transforming the fundamental structures that generate those crises. The crossing point—what could be a threshold to dimensional breakthrough—instead becomes merely another turn in an endless circuit of endurance.

Within this flattening, resilience becomes not liberation but accommodation—the capacity to withstand increasing pressure without challenging the **Master's House** itself. Organizations celebrate "resilient employees" who can absorb mounting workloads without breaking. Communities are praised for their "resilience" in recovering from disasters without questioning the systems that made them vulnerable. Marginalized groups are admired for their "resilience" in navigating hostile environments rather than transforming those environments.

Breaking the Loop in Upstate New York

My work against fracking in upstate New York illustrates how someone might navigate beyond this resilience trap. When the natural gas industry advanced into rural communities, the conventional resilience narrative suggested only two options: adapt to the industry's presence by negotiating better terms, or resist through protest while preparing to recover from inevitable environmental impacts.

Both options represented movement along the same figure-eight pattern—adaptation without transformation, recovery without fundamental change. The communities were expected to demonstrate resilience either by accommodating extraction or by developing recovery strategies for its aftermath.

Rather than accepting this dimensional limitation, I developed what I call *Stereographic Intelligence*, an alternative approach to resilience. As a former corporate attorney, I recognized how legal frameworks created the appearance of inevitability—processes where communities could express concerns but ultimately had to accept state authority over energy development.

Instead of merely helping communities endure this process, I identified a hidden dimensional possibility within existing legal frameworks. By repurposing municipal zoning ordinances—tools conventionally used to promote development—I helped communities create legal protections against extraction altogether. What appeared from conventional perspectives as ordinary zoning became, in practice, a profound reconfiguration of legal authority and community sovereignty.

This approach wasn't merely adaptation or resistance within the industry's parameters but transformation of the parameters themselves. It wasn't about becoming more resilient within the extraction economy but about changing the fundamental relationship between communities, governance, and the extractors.

Reflection

Identify Your Loops: What recurring challenges in your life or organization follow a figure-eight pattern? Where do you find yourself developing better coping mechanisms rather than transforming the underlying conditions?

Seeing Through the Crossing Point

The ∞ lemniscate offers another profound insight when viewed from a three-dimensional perspective. What appears as a crossing point in two dimensions doesn't actually intersect in three dimensions—one path passes over the other without collision. The apparent conflict or contradiction exists only when our perception is dimensionally constrained.

This geometric insight illuminates how genuine resilience involves not just navigating challenges but perceiving them differently—seeing through the apparent crossing points to recognize dimensional possibilities beyond them. The problem isn't so much the challenge itself but the dimensional limitations through which we perceive the challenge.

Recall that in the **Master's House**, resilience is co-opted into a containment strategy—allowing systems of domination to perpetuate because those within them become proficient at tolerating harm. Communities develop extraordinary capacities to absorb shock, adapt to disruption, and recover from trauma, but these very capacities can inadvertently sustain the very **Master's House**, causing harm.

Transformative resilience requires what I call *Stereographic Intelligence*—the capacity to perceive *volumetric* possibilities where *flat* [low resolution] thinking sees only surface limitations. This involves recognizing that what appears as an inevitable collision or repetition may be an artifact created by dimensional compression.

My approach embodied this *Stereographic Intelligence*. Where conventional legal thinking saw only a flat landscape of state preemption over local control, I perceived a dimensional possibility—a legal ecology where community authority could create protected spaces within the **Master's House**. My dimensional perception revealed pathways that conventional frameworks couldn't recognize.

Reflection

Examine Dimensional Constraints: What situations appear as unavoidable conflicts or contradictions from your current perspective? How might these look different if viewed through a three-dimensional lens?

Stereographic Intelligence: Beyond Binary Response

At the heart of transformative resilience lies *Stereographic Intelligence*— the capacity to hold multiple frequencies simultaneously rather than oscillating between binary polarities. Like a musical chord that combines three distinct notes to create something more than the sum of its parts, *Stereographic Intelligence* enables responses that transcend the limitations of either/or thinking.

Conventional resilience oscillates between resistance and accommodation, between fighting systems and adapting to them. This binary oscillation keeps us trapped within the infinite lemniscate loop, perpetually returning to the same crossing points. *Stereographic Intelligence* introduces a third-dimensional element— transformation that encompasses and transcends both resistance and accommodation.

We can understand this through the metaphor of a musical triad:

- The root (fundamental) represents grounding in current reality—acknowledging constraints and immediate needs
- The third (mediating tone) represents adaptation— developing capacities to navigate challenges
- The fifth (harmonic catalyst) represents transformation— generating possibilities beyond current parameters

Only when in accord [a chord] do these elements create a vessel capable of holding genuine transformation. Binary responses— oscillating between just two tones—create unstable intervals rather than coherent chords. Polarity leaves us trapped in the resilience-as-endurance loop rather than opening dimensional gateways beyond it.

My approach to the fracking challenge embodied this harmonic approach to intelligence. I grounded communities in current reality (acknowledging the immediate threat), developed adaptive capacities (using existing legal tools), and catalyzed transformation (fundamentally altering the relationship between local and state authority). My work wasn't merely adaptation or resistance but a third possibility that transcended both—a dimensional shift in how governance itself functioned.

Reflection

Assess Binary Patterns: Where do you find yourself oscillating between resistance and accommodation? How might introducing a third element—transformation —change your approach?

From Endurance to Emergence: Resilience as Threshold Crossing

True resilience isn't about returning to previous states but about evolving to higher complexity through disruption. Like water heated to its boiling point, systems at certain thresholds don't merely intensify—they transform qualitatively, reorganizing at higher orders of complexity and possibility.

The crossing point in the infinite ∞ lemniscate—what conventional resilience interprets as a challenge to be overcome—actually represents a threshold between dimensions. It's not merely a disruption to endure but a gateway to breakthrough, not a crossing to navigate but a portal to transcend.

Stereographic Intelligence transforms how we understand resilience itself. Rather than the capacity to maintain function despite disruption, resilience becomes the capacity to use disruption as a catalyst for dimensional expansion. The most resilient systems aren't those that return to previous states most quickly but those that evolve most coherently through threshold crossings.

My work demonstrates this evolutionary resilience. The communities facing fracking didn't merely recover from disruption—they evolved through it, developing new capacities for governance, sovereignty, and ecological relationship. The threat became not just a challenge to survive but a threshold to cross, not just a crisis to endure, but a portal to a different configuration of possibility.

What began as local ordinances protecting specific communities evolved into a statewide movement that fundamentally transformed New York's approach to extraction. This evolution wasn't merely an adaptation at increasing scale but a dimensional shift in how governance itself functions—what complexity theorists might call "phase transition" to a higher order.

Reflection

Recognize Threshold Moments: What current disruptions in your life, community, or organization might represent thresholds rather than obstacles? What qualitative transformation might be possible if viewed as portals?

Beyond Reframing: Presence as Generation

Conventional resilience often focuses on *reframing* challenges—developing new perspectives that make difficulties more manageable. While valuable, *reframing* remains a two-dimensional response—adjusting perspectives within existing parameters rather than transforming the parameters themselves.

Transformative resilience moves beyond reframing to what we might call "presence as generator"—embodying the consciousness that creates new frames altogether rather than merely modifying existing ones. It involves recognizing ourselves not as beings adapting to pre-existing realities but as participating in the field of reality's continuous creation.

This generative presence doesn't deny current constraints, but neither does it accept them as definitive. It holds the paradox of working within limitations while simultaneously transforming them—not through superhuman effort but through *Stereographic Intelligence* that perceives possibilities invisible to flattened [polarized] awareness.

I embodied this generative presence when I approached municipal law not as a fixed constraint but as a creative medium, not as a rigid boundary but as a dimensional possibility. I didn't merely help communities adapt to legal frameworks; I transformed what those frameworks meant and how they functioned. My approach wasn't just a clever strategy but an ontological revolution—changing not just what communities did but what governance itself could be.

Reflection

Evaluate Reframing Habits: How often do you respond to challenges by reframing them within existing parameters rather than generating new frameworks altogether?

Conclusion: Resilience Reconsidered

As we face cascading ecological, social, and technological disruptions, resilience will remain an essential capacity for individuals, communities, and systems. Yet how we understand this capacity will profoundly shape whether it functions as a mechanism of containment or a catalyst for transformation.

Resilience-as-endurance keeps us trapped in the lemniscate infinity loop—adapting to increasing pressures without transforming the **Master's House** generating those pressures. Resilience-as-emergence enables us to recognize thresholds as dimensional gateways—opportunities to evolve beyond current enclosure into new configurations of possibility.

Developing this evolutionary regenerative resilience requires more than improved coping mechanisms or recovery strategies. It demands *Stereographic Intelligence*—the capacity to perceive volumetric possibilities where polarized thinking sees only surface limitations, to recognize apparent contradictions as gateways to higher integration, to embody generative presence that transforms parameters rather than merely adapting to them.

As we navigate the crossing points in our personal and collective journeys, we face a profound choice. We can continue developing extraordinary capacities to endure within the **Master's House**, becoming ever more skilled at traversing the recursive loop. Or we can cultivate the *Stereographic Intelligence* that transforms those crossing points from challenges to be overcome into thresholds to be crossed—from moments of crisis to portals of emergence.

True resilience isn't about bouncing back. It's about breaking patterns—recognizing that what appears as inevitable return may actually be a dimensional gateway to possibilities beyond our current imagination.

Apply

Map Crossing Points: Identify a recurring challenge in your community or organization. Rather than devising better navigation strategies, explore how this crossing point might serve as a gateway to systemic transformation.

Create Protected Spaces: Where might existing structures or processes be repurposed to create zones of possibility within seemingly hostile environments? Start with a small-scale experiment.

Cultivate Generative Presence: Practice approaching constraints not as fixed limitations but as creative boundaries. Spend time in contemplation before responding to challenges, allowing new possibilities to emerge rather than defaulting to familiar patterns.

Erica Elliott

WarriorHeart Healing Hearts, LLC
Counselor, Coach, Speaker, Author, Consultant

https://www.linkedin.com/in/erica-elliott-ms-lpc-b90911150
https://www.facebook.com/warriorheartxo
https://www.instagram.com/warriorheartxo
https://msha.ke/warriorheartxo
https://linktr.ee/WarriorHeartxo

I possess a Master's Degree in Counseling Psychology and have invested over three decades in my career as a Licensed Counselor, Certified Brain Health Coach, and Certified Health Integrative Medicine Professional. My expertise encompasses a broad spectrum of therapeutic approaches, such as Neurobiology, ADHD and Neurodiversity, Somatic Therapy, Energy Medicine, NLP, CBT, RET, EFT, TFT, Theology, EMDR, the Gottman Method, alongside Mindfulness and Meditation. I am an author and spent over a decade in the military. I am the owner of WarriorHeart Healing Hearts where I champion a comprehensive healing philosophy that harmonizes the mind, body, and spirit. I help individuals clear up the mess to discover their MASTERPIECE using a combination of healing modalities to rapidly rewire for success! Throughout my career, I've had the privilege of helping thousands of individuals, viewing my work not merely as a profession but as a calling. I am truly passionate about empowering others to grow, heal, and soar, unlocking the incredible life that God has always envisioned for them. Having navigated my own share of trials, traumas, and triggers, I deeply understand that healing flourishes through compassionate relationships. Together, we cultivate resilience and vitality, transforming legacies. Like iron sharpening iron, if you're looking for support or just want to connect, you were destined for greatness! Be Blessed and Be a Blessing!

Discovering My Place in the World

By Erica Elliott

Do you ever contemplate your place in the world? Before age eight, my great-grandmother lived in a trailer house next to us. She was the most wonderful, godly woman. I always say she was like what I imagine Mother Teresa was like, just the way that she treated you. You felt very loved. After she moved away, I felt like a solitary figure navigating through a world where everyone else seemed to effortlessly and confidently know their place. My upbringing was profoundly shaped by my grandparents, who played an instrumental role in my formative years. As a result, I often found myself donning hand-me-downs from the church—garments that reflected the lives and stories of those who gave them away, not feeling connected to my identity or having a say in what I preferred. The teasing and bullying I endured from my peers became an all-too-familiar backdrop to my childhood, a constant reminder that I was different, perhaps even somewhat unwanted or foreign. In the midst of this emotional turmoil, I discovered a sanctuary in my adventurously creative mind. I could find myself lost in the clouds above me as I captured images of the stories the clouds told. Frequently, I sought refuge atop our two-story barn, lying flat on my back and gazing up at the expansive sky, allowing my imagination to wander freely. I would conjure fantastical shapes from the drifting clouds and engage in heartfelt conversations with God, the animals that roamed the farm, or simply let my mind drift into whimsical adventures far removed from the confines of my life.

In those precious moments of solitude, I often daydreamed about a life where my biological parents would come to my rescue and whisk me away from the hardships and struggles that filled my daily existence. I envisioned a world overflowing with love, stability, and acceptance, a stark contrast to the chaotic reality I was living in. My days were often spent exploring the vast expanses of the farm, on a quest for the perfect rocks along the road or in the massive creeks, hoping to uncover hidden treasures such as arrowheads or rose rocks. I still vividly remember the day I stumbled upon a toy from a gumball machine, an artifact that had somehow survived from the era of World War I—its presence serving as a unique punctuation mark in my otherwise ordinary existence.

Growing up on a farm with Grandparents who came from the harsh era of the Dust Bowl, my grandparents instilled in me the importance of finishing every morsel on my plate, even if it meant enduring the horrible taste of liver. The memories of those meals linger in my mind, a grotesque reminder of the long hours spent at the dining table, battling my gag reflex while desperately wishing I could hide the reminiscence of it. My childhood was marked by this ongoing struggle between survival and a deep yearning for something greater, something beyond the confines of my challenging circumstances. I witnessed many people around me in the church who seemed to have a different life, more loving and freer.

I often found myself lost in thought, pondering the motivations behind people's actions and the paths they chose to take. Even before I embarked on my journey to become a counselor, I carried this innate curiosity within me. I would frequently ask my grandfather about his childhood, piecing together the puzzle of his past and striving to understand the roots of his abusive behavior. This quest for understanding often led me to feel a deep sense of empathy for him, especially as I uncovered the layers of his complex story where he was abused as well. My grandmother, however, represented a different conundrum altogether. Raised in a nurturing environment, she was spoiled yet cruel, and her behavior perplexed me as a child. Even then, I began to recognize the complexities of human behavior and how the absence of boundaries could cultivate a sense of entitlement.

One pivotal event occurred when I was ten years old, as I found myself in an unusual competition with a boy in my class—a contest to see who could endure the most licks from the school principal. It was an odd pursuit for most girls, but I was determined to excel and prove myself. During my time in the principal's office, he uttered a statement that would resonate as a profound enlightenment in my life: "Erica, I know your family, but you don't have to be a product of your family." His words struck me like a bolt of lightning, illuminating a flicker of hope within me. Although I returned home to the same environment, that single conversation planted a seed of possibility within my heart and mind, urging me to envision a future that was not dictated by my past or my family.

In my quest for guidance, I frequently turned to God in prayer, seeking clarity and direction in a world that often felt chaotic and overwhelming. My struggles with reading were particularly frustrating; my mind would wander, leaving paragraphs unread, and daunting fear that I was missing something. Yet, a powerful glimmer of determination fired up within me. I longed to be different, to carve out a path that diverged from the shadows of what I knew and experienced of my family's history. As I read stories in my search for something to guide me, I became something of a detective, much like the *Nancy Drew* and *Hardy Boys* series. I sought answers, driven by an insatiable desire to uncover what it truly meant to thrive in a world filled with challenges.

Church became my sanctuary, a refuge where I felt a connection to something greater than myself. My early experiences within the church were a mixed bag, filled with both fear and solace. The first congregation I attended preached fire and brimstone, instilling a deep-seated fear within my young heart. I remember trembling at the thought of needing to repent for sins I didn't even comprehend. However, I eventually discovered communities filled with love, acceptance, and genuine care. As I grew older, my curiosity led me to explore different denominations, asking questions and gathering insights about their beliefs and practices. My quest for spiritual understanding became akin to a detective's pursuit of truth, and I embraced it wholeheartedly.

When I turned eleven, a significant shift occurred in my life when my grandparents relocated to Chicago. I spent a month living with a great aunt and my great-grandmother in Illinois, where I attended yet another church. This experience was enlightening, revealing the vast spectrum of beliefs and practices upheld by different congregations. Upon returning to live with my grandparents, I found myself residing in a trailer court, a far cry from the expansive farmlands of my youth. The noise and chaos of urban life felt foreign to me, and I grappled with a sense of dislocation amidst all the unfamiliar faces and surroundings, yet it was also exciting and freeing. I was new here and no one knew me. So, a part of me was feeling a wonderment that this place would be different, better.

As I rode my bicycle through the streets, I encountered a group of children who posed a shocking question: "Do you do drugs?" The inquiry sent a chill down my spine; I had never encountered such a concept before, and it filled me with confusion and apprehension. Fear gripped me, and I hesitated to share my concerns with anyone, worried that revealing my vulnerability might hinder my chances of making friends. My entry into fifth grade marked the beginning of an experiential new chapter, complete with computers—an entirely novel experience for a girl raised in the country. While I felt both intrigued and intimidated, I clung to the hope that life would improve and that I would find my way in this new environment. I learned how to ride a skateboard and ride my ten-speed with no hands, something I could have never learned on our country backroads. Despite the excitement of the new friends and many new things I learned, it was all short-lived, and by the next semester, I was moved back home to live back in the country with my aunt and uncle.

The only solace was that I cherished the aunt and uncle I moved in with, and later in my teenage years, moved in with them permanently. They provided a nurturing, supportive environment, and my aunt, an avid reader and role model for me. I admired her strength, intelligence, and independence, and I yearned to emulate her in more ways than one. I knew she spent hours every night reading. Maybe that's the difference I pondered.

Determined to excel in my studies, I began to read voraciously, even if it meant skimming through pages to grasp the essence of various stories. Each book became a portal to new adventures, dreams, and infinite possibilities. One incredible day, I stumbled upon a life-changing book: Norman Vincent Peale's *The Power of Positive Thinking*. It was as though a light had been ignited within me, illuminating paths I had never considered before and offering me a new perspective on life. Could this be what I was looking for? Does it hold the keys to something better? I had to try the exercises within. What did I have to lose? No one else was giving me guidance. Other than the Bible, it was the first thing I had read that felt like it was literally guiding my soul to something better.

I vividly remember being in seventh or eighth grade, feeling a surge of hope and inspiration as I absorbed the lessons from Peale's book. I took a cassette recorder and a cassette that I had placed tape over the bottom so I could record over it and began documenting my aspirations, listening to my recorded hopes every night before bed. To my astonishment, everything I wished for began to materialize— except for one particular item, which ultimately proved to be a blessing in disguise. This experience ignited within me a fervent passion for manifesting my dreams, a powerful tool that I would carry into adulthood, shaping my beliefs and actions for years to come. Giving me a taste of how the brain and visualization work. Creating within me a fascination and deep desire to learn more about the brain and how we work.

Throughout my journey in life, I sought knowledge and guidance from various sources. As a counselor for over thirty years, I learned from experts and coaches, continually honing my skills to help others navigate their own paths. I realized that life is fundamentally a journey of discovery, where each individual possesses the power to shape their own destiny. It is imperative to recognize our uniqueness and embrace it, allowing ourselves to express our true selves without causing harm to others.

In the past several years since my divorce, I began delving deeper into what I want my life to reflect as I guide my daughter and change the legacy. Reflecting on my myriad experiences, I often find myself asking, *What truly lights me up?* and *What do I genuinely want in life?* Always asking God to lead and guide me. These introspective questions have become guiding principles, steering me toward a more fulfilling existence. I have witnessed the transformative power of manifestation and the profound impact it can have on our lives. I've learned that clarity is paramount; without it, we risk losing sight of our goals amidst the noise and distractions of everyday life.

Four years ago, my life took an unexpected and challenging turn when I fell gravely ill. The toll of years spent neglecting my body's needs finally caught up with me. I had manifested numerous achievements—modeling for magazines, publishing songs, leadership, creating programs to train counselors, and helping thousands of people heal, grow, glow, and soar. Yet, my body, like an overworked Mack Truck, eventually broke down. During my recovery, I sought to understand how I had manifested this. I came to realize that clarity and prioritization are essential to living a balanced and fulfilling life. I manifested what I continued to focus and strive towards, but I had far too much on my plate and had learned early in life how to be a workaholic. Until my body failed, a gift in itself, although I am still healing, gave me a taste of an easier, more beautiful, balanced, blessed, and abundant life. Since I not only have a greater understanding of how to manifest an abundantly blessed life, but also much quicker and easier than ever before. You can find more about the tools God has taught me in the book I wrote, *Breath of Heaven – Manifesting God's Way*", using Biblical Laws and Brain Science to Create an Abundantly Blessed Life. How my husband and I bought a yacht and traveled the ocean for a year, how I became a

USA best-selling author, and how I'm in Belize writing what you just read, living beyond my dreams, the most blessed, abundant life.

As I navigated the arduous path to healing, I understood that our bodies are not meant to function like machines; they are instruments that deserve respect, love, and care. The more attuned I became to my physical and emotional needs, the more my dreams began to unfold in miraculous and unexpected ways. Each day, I express gratitude to God for the countless blessings in my life, recognizing that this journey is not solely for my benefit—it's a gift intended for all who seek to embrace it.

God desires to bless your life, too. He yearns to reveal the abundance that awaits you, ready to unfold in your own life story. All you need to do is ask, clarify your desires, and remain attentive to your body's signals and your intuition. As you embark on this transformative journey, remember to rest when needed, listen to your instincts, and seek alignment with your true purpose and passions.

I invite you to explore your own path, to engage in self-discovery and reflection. What ignites your passion? What dreams have you tucked away in the corners of your heart, waiting to be realized? Join me on this transformative journey, and together, let's uncover the masterpiece that lies within you, waiting to be expressed. If my story resonates with you, I encourage you to visit my website, where you'll find guided meditations and resources designed to support your journey of self-discovery, healing, and manifestation. Imagine soaring in your life's purpose and abundance as you dive deep in my Masterpiece God Centered Mastery Coaching Course using the 777 Method God gave me to clearly soar in life.

Be blessed and be a blessing to others, until we meet again.

Adrian Gentilcore

Your Fairy Techmother
Entrepreneur

https://linkedin.com/in/adrian-gentilcore
https://facebook.com/yourfairytechmotherva
https://instagram.com/yourfairytechmotherva
https://yourfairytechmother.com/
https://yourfairydebtmother.com/

Adrian Gentilcore is a seasoned entrepreneur with a 40-year career in Corporate America and a proven track record of creating successful online businesses. Now a full-time freelancer, she operates two distinct brands: Your Fairy Debtmother, where she offers her expertise as a Debt-Free Coach and popular Personal Finance Blogger and Your Fairy Techmother, where she specializes as a LinkedIn Trainer, Email Marketer, and Web Designer. In her 60s, Adrian has embraced the spirit of feminism and is interested in empowering other midlife women to step into their power and embrace their formidable abilities.

A Sideways Love Story

By Adrian Gentilcore

So, to start with the facts, I grew up as an illegitimate child. In about 1955, my mother started having an affair with a married co-worker. Then, on New Year's Eve 1960, she got pregnant with me.

In modern times, this would be a life-changing situation, but in the 60s in a conservative community of Salt Lake City, this was a tsunami. And it was a tsunami with many unusual twists and turns that changed all our lives in big and small ways.

In my last book collaboration, I wrote about how women are getting a raw deal in every area of life, and an out-of-wedlock pregnancy is probably the ultimate life circumstance where women bear 99% of the impact.

The really depressing thing is that more than six DECADES later, things haven't changed very much. Yes, we've done away with *MOST* of the stigma and scandal. But even now, women are still bearing nearly 100% of the physical, emotional, financial, and life-impacting responsibility for the child, while men have a mostly optional role.

Just ask any pregnant teenager. She is visibly and uncomfortably pregnant while the father has complete freedom to deny, ignore, and even humiliate her. And has no legal or financial responsibility unless his parentage is proven by DNA testing. Not to mention the risk to her life during childbirth if she chooses to have the baby, and in today's environment, she often doesn't have any other choice.

During the Pregnancy

But back to the original dilemma of my mom and dad. Some of the details are pretty fuzzy, and at this point, most of the people who knew are long dead. But as I've gotten older, I've given a lot of thought to what her life must've been like, and I've gained tremendous respect for what she must have gone through to have me and raise me as an unwed mother.

It's not clear what happened in the workplace as neither of them ever spoke of it. Typically, the woman would have been immediately fired, but I wonder if she managed to pull off a fake marriage or some other good cover story. We probably will never know, but I'm sure it was no picnic.

My mom also had a 12-year-old daughter from a previous abusive marriage that she was already raising on her own. The family didn't seem to turn their backs on her, which was not typical of those days. But my grandparents had had a scandal of their own in the early 40s when my grandmother left an alcoholic husband to run off with another man. She managed to get a divorce (rare in those days) and married my mom's stepfather, so maybe they were a bit more understanding.

The only thing Mom ever mentioned about that time is that her stepfather mentioned the idea of an abortion just once, and she never forgave him for it. Abortions weren't legal then or easy to come by, but they were possible, so I'm glad she held her ground and insisted on having me.

My father's marriage was more than a little unusual. His wife had a serious mental illness that had been hidden from him prior to the marriage – back then, it was called paranoid schizophrenia, and treatments were considerably less effective in that time.

I understand that she was confined to a medical facility at times and doesn't seem to have been living a normal, healthy life the rest of the time. They had no children and a barely functional marriage from what I can gather. I never met her, but my mom mentioned some angry phone calls from her, so apparently, she had some knowledge of the affair.

Not that it excuses the illicit relationship, but I can see my father's side of it. He would be a cad to divorce a severely ill wife, but also a cad for not marrying the mother of his child. So, he was just kind of neutral, like Switzerland.

He never told his parents that I even existed, which was a shame as his brother had all sons. They might have enjoyed having a granddaughter. I did get to meet my uncle and cousins when I was much older, and I enjoyed that, as I was hungry for family connection. I still interact with my cousins on Facebook.

My dad was an okay guy – we certainly could have done much worse. He never drank, smoked, or cussed, never yelled or raised a hand to me or my mother. He had few friends – mostly golf buddies and didn't really have close relationships with anyone other than my mother and possibly his wife.

Kids – he just didn't get them, not me, my sister, or the grandkids. He'd kind of pat you on the head and then ignore you until you went away. I think he might have been a little on the spectrum. He liked dogs and cats and told bad golf jokes.

When I Was Born

Fast-forward to baby time. When I was born, my mother at first *refused* to see me because I was a girl – she demanded that they bring in her SON. You see, she'd been holding out a secret hope that my dad might marry her if she managed to come up with a *boy* to carry on his family name.

I'm pretty sure that's why she gave me a boy's name – Adrian – and insisted that she couldn't have had a daughter. She did relent after an hour or so and was always an extremely good mother to me from then on. We had very similar personalities and got along very well as I was growing up.

I like my name, but I think I felt subtle pressure to be more like a boy than a girl. I've always felt like I was much more masculine-leaning than feminine.

She somehow convinced my father to sign the birth certificate, but apparently, she was terrified to ask him for money, and he didn't offer any financial support. She finally HAD to ask him for a modest amount of money when I was about 12, but up until then, it was just us three on whatever she could scrape together.

But Mom was very smart with money. Even though she had a basic clerical job, she managed to pay for a house in a nice neighborhood, a car, and all the basic necessities for two growing girls. That's pretty amazing and would be nearly impossible in today's economy for a single woman.

I look at my few baby pictures and I think about how difficult her life must've been. Two kids to provide for, very little family support – my grandmother died of esophageal cancer when I was 6, and my mom had to nurse her as well for the last year or two.

I think of every nighttime feeding, every diaper, every bottle – all on her own, while holding down a job, sometimes a couple of them. I'm guessing there wouldn't have been a baby shower, and I can't imagine people wanting to admire and hold her new baby, given the circumstances, that would have been as welcome as handing them a live hand grenade. It must have been hurtful for her.

Obviously, it is not my fault, but I can see where it would have been a little weird. I don't remember my grandparents well, but I can't imagine they would have been too pleased by having living proof of an extramarital affair running around their house.

It was especially hard on my older sister. She detested my dad, rightfully so, after all the scandal and uproar their relationship caused. It's hard to keep secrets in a small town, so neighborhood kids weren't allowed to come to our house, and I'm sure all the mothers in the neighborhood felt sorry for her for living in such a sinful household.

My sister reports that they moved around a lot. Sometimes to California to be near my dad, sometimes back to Utah to care for my grandmother. I suspect they also had to move sometimes because some old biddy had found out the secret around my birth and was raising a stink. My sister went to many different schools and had trouble making friends, even though she was very bright and outgoing.

Big Changes Happening Fast

My sister ended up pregnant just after high school and got married at the age of 17 when I was just 5. In the oddest coincidence, my nephew was born, my grandmother died, and I started kindergarten all on the exact same day – September 6, 1966!

My sister's husband had enlisted in the Navy, and she moved to San Diego to be with him. Shortly thereafter, my mother, who was heartbroken after the death of her mother, packed me into her turquoise DeSoto and moved us into an apartment in Long Beach, a few blocks from my father's office.

She also had a lifelong friend who lived nearby – a divorced cat lady who eventually became an alcoholic. She became my adopted grandmother, and when I was in my teens, I'd drive her to the grocery store every week and sit and talk to her for hours.

Most of the time, it was just Mom and me. My dad would come by every Saturday, and they would take me with them to the laundromat and the grocery store. Then, we'd have lunch at a diner nearby. We'd go home and they'd put me down for a nap, so they could have a little time alone.

It wasn't a bad childhood. A bit lonely, as I had no siblings and few friends, no aunts, uncles, or cousins around. But it was quiet and peaceful, which is a wonderful way to raise a child. Mom would come home from work, pop two TV dinners in the oven, and we would watch TV, and read or do crafts until bedtime. This was our routine pretty much every day of the week.

I only realized this just recently, but I believe my mom had become agoraphobic (a fear of the outdoors). I never thought of it before because there were places that we HAD to go – bank, grocery store, doctor, laundromat, and, of course, work and school, but otherwise, we rarely left the house even for a walk around the block or a trip to the playground. We had almost no friends or family in the area other than her cat lady friend.

I think that's why I was the exact opposite with my kids. We had a big church family and planned big birthday parties, took them to carnivals, zoos, circuses, anything going on in town. We also had them involved in Scouts, youth group, and every other activity I could manage. I'd even save my vacation days to attend school field trips or activities with our church youth group or Scout Troop.

But my mom taught me how to read at a young age and bought me my first of many kittens for my 6th birthday. She was kind and very easy-going. She tried to be strict, but it wasn't really in her nature. Fortunately, I was a fairly compliant child, so I rarely caused her any trouble.

My Teen Years

Oddly enough, no one ever told me I was an illegitimate child when I was growing up. The cover story was that my parents were divorced, and since I didn't know any better, I accepted that completely. How would I know that divorced couples rarely date?

My mom finally filled in the blanks when I was in high school. By then, I had developed a bit of a complex. I never really understood why everyone in my family seemed to dislike me, other than my mother.

When the people who are most important in your life don't seem to like you, it has a big impact on your self-worth. I became extremely self-conscious of everything about myself.

You start to question everything. Are you not pretty enough, nice enough, smart enough (or in my case, too smart)? Clearly, something was dreadfully wrong with me since my mother and a few teachers were the only ones who seemed to like me.

In most kids, this would have made them very shy and lacking in confidence. But I flipped the script. I figured if they didn't like me, I would do everything I possibly could to MAKE them like me.

So, I became a toxic overachiever – I was the best reader in first grade, emceed the school talent show at the ripe old age of 7. I didn't get straight A's, but I did very well without much effort in every subject but math.

In fact, I got such good grades that I started Community College at 16, focusing on performing arts – theater, music, dance, stage management, lighting design – I did it ALL until I was hit by a drunk driver when I was 18 and had to drop out.

I badly wanted to get a job, so I got my work permit the minute I turned 14 and got my first part-time job immediately thereafter. I've pretty much worked every day since then, often working a full-time job and a side hustle while raising 3 kids. I was a textbook workaholic.

Oddly enough, my sister also turned out to be a workaholic – she's still working part-time well into her 70s. I think something about growing up with a single mom made a huge impression on us about how precarious life can be, so we both became obsessed with overachieving at work to support our families. None of us had a college degree, except my father, but we all did very well in mid-level careers.

I was very uneasy about calling out sick. Taking even a sick day was hugely guilt-ridden for me – I had at least one 5-year stretch where I didn't take a single sick day. Even now, when I've had cancer twice, I work pretty much every day. I think it didn't feel "safe" to take time off work because that could have jeopardized Mom's job, and our lives would have collapsed like a house of cards.

One thing my mother did very well was teach us how to manage money. She taught my sister how to handle all the bills when she was pretty young and had me pay rent by the time I was 16. Sounds harsh, but she needed the help, and it was the best lesson I ever had about being responsible with money.

I lived at home until I got married at 24. I insisted that both parents walk me down the aisle because I felt my mom deserved that honor much more than my dad, but I didn't want to shame him because he was footing the bill.

The next year, we got a bit of a shock. My father's wife passed away after a brief illness.

By then, I was 25 and my parents had been "dating" for more than 30 years. That's pretty wild. Mom had tried to leave him a couple of times, but it never stuck, and they would get back together.

A few weeks later, my mom said he just showed up at her door with a suitcase and his cat in a carrier, and just like that, they moved in together and started planning a very belated wedding.

They got married in my cousin's living room with my sister as the maid of honor and me as a bridesmaid. I've got a lot of pictures from that day and they both look so happy.

They both retired and bought a comfortable house in Salt Lake City with a big yard. They traveled a lot, and my dad played golf every week. My sister and I both lived nearby with our families, so they had frequent chances to spend time with the whole family, which was a lot of fun. My mom was a terrific grandmother and really enjoyed the grandkids without spoiling them too much.

They had a happy seven years together before my dad passed. It was quite a unique love story, but I'm so happy my mom had her happy ending at last.

Lessons Learned

I learned a lot from my childhood and this unusual situation. I've taken after my mother in many ways but also made some deliberate choices to go my own way. Here are some lessons I've learned from her:

- It may take decades to get the happy ending, but if you are positive, patient, and hopeful, things will eventually work out in your favor.

- No matter what, enjoy your children. So many parents seem to dislike their children, and no wonder. They allow them to behave like little jerks. Your kids are going to be living with you for at least 18 years. Raise them to be people you enjoy having around. My mom wasn't very strict, but she didn't put up with any shenanigans either.

- Give your kids the gift of responsibility. Self-sufficient kids tend to grow up into self-sufficient adults.

- Do what is best for you, even if it makes people unhappy. Waiting a lifetime for a man may not have been the right strategy for everyone, but it was her choice.

- Family is important. Stick by them if you can, but if you can't, good friends make wonderful substitutes.

- Don't underestimate your own abilities. Yes, it's nice to have help from a partner, but a woman should always have money in their own name, and the means to leave the relationship if necessary. Save part of every paycheck – even in retirement. Rainy days are GOING to happen.

- It doesn't cost much to be kind to people – my mom took great delight in sending little gifts to friends and family members who were down on their luck, and opened her home to several family members who needed a place to stay.

- Have some fun – even on a tight budget. Your kids will remember playing a card game with you and toasting marshmallows much more than a trip to Disneyland or an expensive vacation.

Michele Gunn

Cultivate and Thrive, She Wins Women's Network
Founder and Self-Actualization Coach, Managing Partner

https://www.linkedin.com/in/michelegunn/
https://www.facebook.com/michele.jonasgunn/
https://www.instagram.com/michelegunn1
www.michelegunn.com
https://shewinswomensnetwork.com/?ref=7

As a Gallup-Certified Strengths Coach and founder of Cultivate and Thrive, Michele Gunn empowers individuals through self-actualization (knowing and embracing self) to embrace their God-given strengths and live purposefully. Since 2018, Michele's faith-based mission has centered on helping people recognize their unique gifts to foster success and fulfillment in all areas of life. Michele's rich experience across family life and various industries brings a wide perspective and deep understanding to her work. A committed Christian, contributing author, and Managing Parter at She Wins Women's network-Houston Chapter, she guides women in building lives rooted in faith and inner strength to thrive in the fulfilling life they were created for. To learn more about Michele and how she can help you embrace all you were created for, connect with her and Cultivate and Thrive on Facebook, Instagram, LinkedIn, or visit her website at www.michelegunn.com.

Steeped in Strength: Embracing Your Unique Blend

By Michele Gunn

The Aroma of Life

Coffee. I love the strong aroma, the warmth, and the comfort it brings. Plain coffee has a distinct aroma that just relaxes me. Starting at the whole bean stage, through the grinding and brewing processes, the smell is fresh and aromatic. The warmth from the brewed cup radiates through my fingers down my hands and up my arms. The cup brings comfort from just holding it in my hands. The steam warms my face as I take in the essence right before I take the first sip. I savor the flavor it provides. It gives me a foundation of strength to start my day!

Hold on! That is just the beginning! There are so many options to enjoy coffee. There are many beans to choose from. There are different ways to brew it. There are many other flavors, syrups, milks, and more you can add to create a unique experience. It can be savored hot or cold. Just like coffee, people are complex, rich, diverse, and created by God. What if we saw ourselves as coffee beans, uniquely crafted by God, with a special purpose to serve? We have the ability to add things or skills to ourselves to enrich us, to make us stronger, sweeter, bolder, and more resilient. We also have the free will to choose wisely or unwisely in all things in life. All of these things create our own unique blend.

Much like how coffee flavors, once combined, can settle and change the experience, you can be settled in life. You may take others for granted, or you may just forget what makes you uniquely magnificent. You may settle for what is left at the bottom instead of enjoying the whole experience. It may be time for a little (or big) stir to bring those flavors back to life. You may need to add a little more flavor. You may need to be reminded of your resilience and uniqueness. You may even need to be brought back to faith. Remember that you were uniquely created for a purpose that is just as unique as you are! Come, discover how you are uniquely made just like a coffee bean, each with its own unique strength! Enjoy some scripture sprinkled in for some added flavor!

Coffee Beans: A Reflection of Humanity

Just like there are many different kinds of coffee beans, there are many different kinds of people. Both were created by God, and both have unique qualities and variations. Don Clifton created an assessment to help us understand the commonalities among themes of human talents. These 34 themes are known as *CliftonStrengths*®. Let's see how some beans symbolize different kinds of people and what *CliftonStrengths*® Talent Themes may be represented in each. Four types of coffee beans are Arabica, Robusta, Liberica, and Excelsa. There are 34 *CliftonStrengths*® Talent Themes.

Arabica beans are grown in tropical regions. They are considered to be the smoother and sweeter beans when compared to others. They are similar to people who bring gentleness and wisdom. You may find people with these CliftonStrengths® here: Arranger®, Connectedness®, Consistency®, Context®, Empathy®, Includer®, Communication®, Developer®, Discipline®, Harmony®, and Positivity®.

Robusta beans are strong and harsh, yet deep in flavor and high in caffeine. These are often used to create instant coffee. Robusta beans are strong, bold, and resilient; much like people who endure hardships with tenacity. You may find people with these CliftonStrengths® here: Achiever®, Belief®, Command®, Learner®, Relator®, and Responsibility®. These themes represent people who strive to get things done using their talents to help find solutions, utilizing people and information.

Liberica beans are much larger than the more popular Arabica and Robusta beans. On a global level, it is rare and in limited supply. These beans are viewed as unique, wild, and unconventional. People who dare to break molds would fit in this category. You may find people with these CliftonStrengths® here: Activator®, Competition®, Ideation®, Individualization®, Restorative®, Self-Assurance®, and Woo®. These talents help to drive success.

Excelsa beans grow mainly in Southeast Asia, where they are used as a blending coffee to add complexity and depth. It has a distinctive, tart, fruity, dark, mysterious taste. It is viewed as complex and multi-layered, much like people who bring depth and introspection. You may find people with these CliftonStrengths® here: Adaptability®, Analytical®, Deliberative®, Focus®, Futuristic®, Input®, Intellection®, Maximizer®, Significance®, and Strategic®. These talents serve the mind and how to find the best way forward.

Just as God creates diverse beans, He creates us each with unique gifts. 1 Peter 4:10 reads, "As each one has received a gift, use it to serve one another as good stewards of God's varied grace." Be open to who you are and the gifts you have. Also, value who other people are and the gifts they bring.

The Brewing Process: The Trials That Shape Us

Different brewing methods represent the challenges and transformations we undergo and how we might handle them. Some of these brewing processes are espresso, French Press, drip coffee, and cold brew. Do any of these resonate with you? Let's dive in!

I do love espresso! Espresso involves intense pressure and quick extraction. This is similar to growth through the high-pressure moments in life. Many people experience traumatic situations or financial hardships. These can be experienced through physical, emotional, health, mental wellness, and relational aspects of life. It could be a lack of love or a lack of self-value. It could be joblessness or a serious injury. Some may face bankruptcy, homelessness, divorce, depression, or many other things. How you pull yourself from these situations, or something similar, is what molds you. These things may help to mold you, but they don't define you.

French Press is a way to truly savor the coffee flavor. It truly allows that coffee flavor to sink into the water. In human life, it is soaking in experience before emerging. It is wisdom gained through patience and experience. When living this way, you are really taking in and enjoying experiences. You are patient, waiting for the outcome. This will bring wisdom through the experiences. It could be wisdom gained for what to do, what not to do, how to do something, or how not to do something. This wisdom gained is for you and for you to share with your unique perspective.

Some people just take things slow and steady, much like the process of drip coffee. Living life with daily faithfulness and perseverance brings a slower, and usually calmer, result. When life is taken at a slower pace, it may be easier to stay on the path you planned, but it may seem like forever to get to the destination. To live this way, the person usually has a lot of patience and can easily see that they are approaching their goals one step (drip) at a time. They may get frustrated at not reaching their destination more quickly, but they enjoy the journey.

Ah, cold brew! This process takes time and patience to extract richness. It is even slower than the drip process. These people are often seen as content with the status quo. In reality, they know where they are headed. They have a plan to reach the desired outcome. People who experience life as a cold brew understand that healing and personal growth take time and are willing to do so. They willingly put in the extra work because they know the outcome they will get and are quite happy to wait for it.

James 1:2-4 reads, "Consider it all joy, my brothers, when you encounter various trials, for you know that the testing of your faith produces perseverance. And let perseverance be perfect, so that you may be perfect and complete, lacking in nothing." Our experiences help to shape us, make us stronger, and develop who we naturally are.

The Perfect Blend: Community and Support

Coffee is rarely consumed alone. It is meant to be shared, just like life! After all, humans were created to be social creatures. We are brought into this world, surrounded by people. Whether it is just family or medical personnel, there are always people present. We go into school systems, social organizations, religious organizations, and work. We look for clubs, sports, and organizations to join. Even self-professed loners are surrounded by people. Donald O. Clifton has been credited with saying, "... our lives are shaped by our interactions with others. Whether we have a long conversation with a friend or simply place an order at a restaurant, every interaction makes a difference."

Like blending different beans creates a unique flavor, coming together strengthens us. We learn from each other. We start with our innate talents and invest in them. We build skills, talents, and knowledge until we have developed a strength. Our interactions also spark new interests (or dull old ones). Sharing information, stories, and emotions guides our growth and helps to shape us. As Donald O. Clifton has said, "Relationships help us to define who we are and what we can become. Most of us can trace our successes to pivotal relationships." Coming together also offers more opportunities to celebrate our wins and to grow and refine our values as we share them with others.

With coffee, there are many things we can add to enhance the flavor experience. Additives can include milk, creamers, a variety of flavored creamers, a variety of sugars and sugar alternatives, and many flavors of syrups and spices. With people, there is a diversity in talents, experiences, cultures, and backgrounds that enrich the world. Know your innate talents to build upon your skills. Find what sparks passion in you to help drive the direction of your growth. Seek opportunities to collaborate with diverse people. Embrace who you are to enrich your life and the life of those you interact with.

Proverbs 27:17 speaks to this, "Iron is sharpened by iron; one person sharpens another." You most likely have heard of the acronym, TEAM. It means, "Together Everyone Achieves More." Having other people around with differing talents is a resource for new knowledge. Other people can also be teachers of new skills. Think about the last time you learned something new in the course of a regular day. Most likely it was because of another person. Be open to learning as well as being open to teaching.

The Purpose of Coffee and Your Purpose: Serving Others

Why do we drink coffee? Coffee tastes good. It fuels us, comforts us, and energizes us. Those who drink it choose to drink it. It is a choice. We are called to serve others much like coffee serves us. We still have to choose to serve. Sometimes, we know what our service or impact will be, and sometimes, we won't even know we made an impact until much later in life. You can still choose to be intentional in serving,

Everything we are, including our experiences, struggles, and triumphs, equips us to pour into other people's lives. Embrace where you have been, the experiences you have had, and the knowledge you have acquired. Embrace your skills and talents. Invest in them. Use those things as fuel (like coffee) to empower you to move forward. Share your stories. Share your knowledge. Share your talents and skills. Serving others is part of who you were created to be. Do it willingly and intentionally.

As women, we are often placed in a box as defined by our roles. For example, a mother, a wife, or the mother of..., the wife of... Then there is the professional role, such as a coach, administrator, lawyer, secretary, etc. Even more simplified are roles put into the box of working mom, stay-at-home mom, single mom, or not a mom. In reality, those are only one part of who you are. You are a whole person, not just the label of what you do for others. Know who you are. Embrace your roles, no matter how big or small. Spend time understanding who you are. Invest in yourself. Celebrate your uniqueness. Celebrate your service to others.

1 Peter 4:10 reminds us, "As each one has received a gift, use it to serve one another as good stewards of God's varied grace." You cannot use your gifts to serve if you do not know what your gifts are. You are worth it and the world needs the you that you were created to be.

Savoring the Journey

Your journey is unique to you. Savor it. Sure, there may be similar stories and similar experiences. There are even shared stories and shared experiences! The fact is, you are unique. Every situation, experience, emotion, challenge, and achievement is uniquely yours because of you! You are that unique addition to life that can sweeten it for others, enrich it, make it bolder, etc. The journey (life) is meant to be enjoyed.

Know yourself. Be you. Own who you are. Embrace yourself, perceived flaws and all! What others may see as flaws are opportunities for growth and collaboration. Enjoy this journey called life. Your uniqueness will not only enrich your life, but it will enrich the lives of others as your life is stirred into the mix with the people you encounter daily. Other people will also enrich your life with the uniqueness they add to the mix, and as they share life with more people.

Be intentionally you, especially in service to others. Life is a journey, and the only time limit put on you for reaching success in service is when this earthly life ends. Even then, your fruits, as well as the seeds you planted (or the beans you grew, harvested, and processed) will still flourish as they are nurtured by the people you have shared them with, stirring in their own, unique flavor.

So, remember, each one of us has a unique journey. Trials and tribulations as well as successes are part of the journey. They will be as unique as each one of us. Know that every trial will refine you, but not define you. Every success will shape you, but not name you. Let success and challenges shape you in a positive way. Find joy in the process, just as you enjoy a cup of coffee. Every add-in, every nuance brings about a new, enticing flavor.

Remember Psalm 34:9, "Taste and see that the Lord is good..." You were created by God. You were created to be unique, to be a blessing to others as well as to be blessed. Go forth, be uniquely bold, be uniquely strong, and pour into others with the unique strength that God has given you.

Embrace your unique blend.

Dedicated with love to Amanda and Taylor, who taught me how to truly enjoy coffee.

Tamsyn Cornelius

Founder of TC Editorial Services
Creative Strategist

https://www.linkedin.com/in/tamsyn-cornelius
https://www.facebook.com/tamsyn.cornelius
https://www.instagram.com/tamsyncornelius_art/
www.tamsyncornelius.com
www.tceditorialservices.co.za

Tamsyn Cornelius is a visionary artist, creative strategist, and retreat curator based in Cape Town, South Africa. As the founder of TC Editorial Services and The TLC Retreat Collective, she blends storytelling with art, faith, and curated creative events to inspire transformation. With a background in content creation, digital communication and magazine editing, Tamsyn helps individuals and brands communicate their stories with clarity and impact. She is passionate about fostering spaces in which others are equipped to reignite purpose and align with their God-given identity. Tamsyn's work spans copywriting and visual art, as well as facilitating creative workshops and retreats which are designed to inspire a global audience to dream boldly and explore authentic expression. Whether through words, visuals, or events, her mission remains the same – to call out the gold in others and help people create, thrive and dream in full colour.

The Courage to Create:
A Journey of Faith and Purpose

By Tamsyn Cornelius

There is a particular kind of courage required to step away from certainty and into a life built on creativity. It is the courage to embrace reinvention and to trust that even when one door closes, another will open if you are willing to step into the unknown...

My journey has never been a straight line but a series of pivots, moments of doubt, and ultimately, a deep commitment to shaping a life aligned to my values.

I was six years old when I realized I wanted to create, even though I didn't really know what that looked like. When my childhood friends were interested in studying medicine, teaching, or law, all I knew for certain was that I wanted a life with the freedom to be creative. Conventional careers did not excite me, and even as a young child, I found myself dreaming up a vocation that I wasn't sure existed. I envisioned a future with pen in hand, scribbles on a page, and the power to create magic on paper.

Creativity often found me in the strangest of places, and like most creatives, I was misunderstood. Instead of traditional childhood games, I found it more satisfying to make up my own. Daydreaming and doodling were my favourite pastimes, and instead of a playroom or doll house, I had my best creative moments in my "secret" getaway, which was under the coffee table in the living room. This was my special place to unpack my colouring pencils and collection of greeting cards and to think up games that would keep me occupied for hours.

Growing up in a traditional, middle-class family in Cape Town, South Africa, creativity was often seen as a hobby, something nice to do in your spare time, but not as a viable career path. The idea of turning artistic expression into a sustainable livelihood seemed far-fetched. The only artists I knew were those whose fame came posthumously—Da Vinci, Matisse, Van Gogh—whose masterpieces were only valued after their deaths. It was hard for me to accept that being creative could only be celebrated when you were no longer around to enjoy it. That wasn't the future I was hoping for.

As I grew older, I searched for a practical way to channel my creativity—something that would allow me to express myself while still being seen as a "real" career. That path led me to journalism. It didn't involve paintbrushes or pastels, but it gave me the next best thing: the ability to craft stories, to shape narratives, to bring words to life.

Fresh out of university, I landed a role as a sub-editor at a local publication—a dream opportunity for a young writer eager to make her mark. Before long, I climbed the ranks to become a magazine editor for a well-established South African publication. The risk had paid off.

Until it didn't.

For a while, it felt like everything I had worked for had fallen perfectly into place. But success on paper does not always translate to fulfilment. The cracks started to show, subtle at first, then impossible to ignore. When the magazine shut down and I was suddenly retrenched and left without a job, I was forced to confront an unsettling truth: life and ambitions could unravel overnight. And if my identity was tied to that role, then who was I without it?

After a season of uncertainty, I found myself asking many questions. Do I try something new or do I settle back into the fast-paced corporate setting I had once known... For some reason, it seemed easier to pursue the corporate career, and I quickly landed a sought-after communications role. But the more I settled in, the clearer it became: this new job offered even fewer opportunities for creative expression than the last. It was a rigid 9-to-5 role in which I quickly began to feel stifled. I was slowly beginning to lose myself and often felt like I was suffocating in an environment that did not align with who I was at my core. The childlike sense of wonder I once had—my big dreams and boundless curiosity—was buried under the weight of routine and monotony.

Then, motherhood came along and changed everything. It reshaped my vision of time, work, and impact. Sitting in my comfy corporate office, pregnant with my first child, I faced a choice: continue on a path that drained me or embrace the unknown yet again. In that moment, I leaned into my faith, trusting that if God had given me this creative spark, He would also guide me in using it for good. I resigned, not because I had a perfect plan, but because I refused to spend my days detached from the purpose He had placed within me.

But here's the truth about stepping away from a career to be home with your children: no matter what you choose, guilt finds a way to creep in. If you stay home, you wonder if you're doing enough, if you're wasting your potential, if you're letting your ambition slip through your fingers. If you work, you wonder if you're missing too much, if your children will resent your absence, if you should be baking cookies instead of answering emails.

I wrestled with both.

Some days, I felt like I had made the bravest decision of my life. Other days, I felt like I had abandoned my identity outside of motherhood. I loved my child fiercely, but I also craved the creative fulfilment that once fuelled me.

When you are knee-deep in dirty laundry and facing sleepless nights, it may feel like this season will never end. But like all phases of life, circumstances change yet again, and a time to pivot is almost always at hand.

That moment arrived three years in, with a four-month-old baby in my arms and a toddler at my feet. I knew it was time to create again—not just for an income, but for me. Slowly, between nap times and late nights, I built something new. I took on small projects, tested ideas, and redefined success on my own terms. And in that messy, chaotic season, I learned some valuable lessons... Motherhood and ambition are not opposites. Choosing your children doesn't mean you have to lose yourself. You can be both present and driven... Both nurturing and ambitious... Both a mother and a creator.

It's not easy. It's never balanced perfectly. But it's possible.

All I knew for sure was that I couldn't go back to how things had been before. The corporate world had given me structure, but it had also stifled me. Creativity wasn't just something I did—it was how I navigated the world, how I solved problems, how I made sense of my place in it.

At first, I struggled to see a way forward. I had always believed that business and creativity lived in separate worlds and that I had to choose between structure and freedom. But as I searched for a way to build a meaningful career without losing my creative spark, I began to wonder: What if I didn't have to choose at all? What if business wasn't just a job but an evolving reflection of who we are, what we value, and how we want to impact the world?

The mindset shift came in waves. The weight of uncertainty was real, and there were moments when I questioned everything. But in that discomfort, I found resilience. I also found God leading me through uncertainty, reminding me that my gifts were not random—they were part of His greater plan. The more I leaned into creativity, the more clarity I gained. At first, it was simply about reclaiming a part of myself I had long neglected. But as I allowed curiosity to guide me, I realized that creativity wasn't just an outlet, it was a compass.

In 2020, as the world came to a standstill, I took it as a challenge to reignite my creative spark. What started as a commitment to paint one piece a month—whether abstract, portrait, or multimedia—soon became a daily practice. As my confidence grew, I began creating with intent, and what was once a personal exploration transformed into a business, offering art and custom products, and later running creative workshops and a kids' art club from home. Each brushstroke, each new project and idea, led me to something bigger—turning self-expression into a thriving venture built on passion and purpose.

Above all, I craved freedom. Not just freedom from rigid career paths but the freedom to evolve, to pivot, to create a life that fit the season I was in. Too often, we build businesses around a single skill, assuming we must stay in one lane forever. But what if we built them around our passions and values instead? A business that grows with us, rather than confines us, has the power to sustain us in ways beyond just financial success.

Motherhood taught me that time is not infinite. Every hour spent chasing success should contribute to a life worth living. The goal isn't just to build a business—it's to build a life that feels aligned with purpose. When we design our creative work to support our vision rather than dictate it, we find more joy in the process.

One of the greatest lessons I've learned is this: Creative entrepreneurship is not static. It thrives in movement, in risk, in reinvention. Don't be afraid to shift, to experiment, to embrace the unknown. The business, the career, the creative work—it should all grow with you.

Many of us were raised to see creativity as optional, as something to pursue only after the "real work" is done. That mindset needs to change. The next generation deserves to see creativity as a foundation—not an afterthought—to build futures, not just hobbies.

People don't just connect with what we create—they connect with why we create it. When our work is rooted in truth, it will almost always outlast trends.

But make no mistake: This path demands resilience. There will be moments of doubt, seasons of struggle, and times when quitting seems easier than continuing. I know this because I've lived it. Losing my job forced me to reimagine success. Stepping away from certainty led me to discover my own voice. The moments that shook my foundation were the very ones that helped to build my future.

For years, I chased the world's definition of security—a steady paycheck, a structured career path, external validation. But true peace came when I surrendered those expectations and stepped fully into the calling placed on my heart. Creativity, faith, and entrepreneurship are not separate pieces of my life; they are interwoven, guiding me toward a life of purpose.

I have learned that when we build a business rooted in who we truly are, we invite joy and meaning into our daily work. When we pursue impact over mere profit, we leave a legacy that outlives us. And when we trust God's plan over our own, we find the courage to step into the unknown, knowing that every season—every success, every failure—is part of something greater.

Today, my life and business continue to evolve. I would not be here without faith, without family, without the unwavering belief that I was created for more. When I doubted myself, I had people who reminded me of my purpose. When I wanted to give up, I leaned into God's plan, even when I couldn't see the next step. And that faith— that trust—is what has carried me through every season.

So, if you find yourself at a crossroads, wondering whether to take the risk, to keep going, to trust your calling—remember this: Your creativity is not an accident. Your gifts were placed within you for a reason. The world needs fresh ideas, and perhaps you and I were called to bring them. Step boldly into who you were meant to be, and trust that the path will unfold in ways you never imagined.

Stacey Dorenfeld

Advocate, Storyteller, Survivor

https://www.linkedin.com/in/stacey-dorenfeld-a678aa347/
https://www.facebook.com/KosherCrack
https://www.instagram.com/koshergirlcracked/

Stacey is a passionate leader and an ardent advocate for change, dedicated to improving the human experience. As the Northern Area President of Hadassah Southern California and a former National Grassroots Advocacy team member, she has collaborated with federal and state representatives to advance human rights initiatives. Stacey's dedication shines through in her efforts to combat antisemitism, condemn Gender Based violence, promote safe gun laws, and advocate for women's reproductive health care. She played an instrumental role in passing legislation to aid victims of human trafficking in California. She was recently recognized with Hadassah's June Walker Advocacy Award for her leadership in Hadassah's Antisemitism: Define, Discuss, Defuse program in 2023. With a degree in communications, Stacey is not only a passionate advocate but also a creative entrepreneur. She has successfully launched two original lines of motivational jewelry, showcasing her innovative spirit. Her professional acumen is evident in her role as the Operations Manager for the family law firm, where she effectively utilizes her organizational skills and unwavering commitment to excellence. A dedicated author, Stacey has shared her voice through three published books and contributions to four anthologies. Her upcoming work, "Kosher Crack," explores the challenging journey of overcoming childhood abuse with depth and sensitivity. She actively engages with her readers on her lifestyle blog, www.koshercrack.com, offering insights and fostering connections. Stacey strives to encourage and influence others through her writing and online presence.

Resilience Isn't a Straight Line:
My Story of Survival, Surrender, and Strength

By Stacey Dorenfeld

Resilience is a word we often hear tossed around—sometimes used to suggest boundless bravery or unbreakable will. But I've learned firsthand that real resilience isn't a shiny badge or a fixed trait. It's messy, quiet, and often, painfully uncertain. It's a quality that grows and changes, emerging in moments you least expect and hiding in places you can't quite see. Most of all, it's not a straight line from hurt to healing. It's a winding path—full of detours, setbacks, and small, but meaningful victories.

I've probably been to six different therapists in my life. Sometimes, I wonder if that is typical for people who've experienced trauma like mine—a sexually abusive stepfather, an absent father, and a drugged-out mother. Maybe it shows just how fiercely I searched for peace and answers. Of those six therapists, I connected with the women I saw best. Perhaps I needed a sense of feminine solidarity— a woman's empathy for what it's like growing up in a home where every day could bring a new reason to be afraid.

The paperwork and co-pays weren't the hard part; it was the telling. Again and again, I had to roll out my life story like a fragile tapestry riddled with holes—assault, substance abuse, family chaos. By the time I reached my fourth therapist, I felt like I was reciting a script. By the sixth, I almost wanted to shove my diary into her hands and say, "Please, just read this so we can finally move on."

Without fail, each time I recounted my story, I braced for that moment when the therapist's eyes would widen. Then they'd say some version of "It's a miracle you're still alive." And I'd nod, feeling a mixture of gratitude, shame, and exhaustion. Because statistically, they wouldn't be wrong. With the childhood I had, it would've been no surprise if I'd ended up on the streets, overdosed, or simply disappeared. Instead, here I am—scraped up but standing. I must have beaten the odds.

Is that resilience?

I feel scrappy. I feel tired. I feel like I've clawed my way through parts of my life with nothing but grit and stubbornness. I've been through things I don't talk about at dinner parties—things I only whisper in therapy rooms.

Even before I knew the word resilience, I understood what it felt like to desperately hope for something better. As a child, I learned to read people's moods the way other kids learn their ABCs—because misreading a shift in atmosphere could mean punishment or worse. My stepfather took advantage of every boundary I had, including my body. My mother, though physically present, was lost in her own fog of pills and needles. We lived in a house of unspoken rules and silent terror.

There were no bedtime stories or safe arms to run to when I was frightened. I taught myself to disappear, to become invisible when tempers flared.

Even so, a tiny spark inside me kept whispering, *Life could be different.* Maybe every kid harbors that hope—that somewhere beyond the abuse, there's a calmer, kinder world. For me, that spark was the seed of resilience.

My biological father was painfully absent. On rare occasions, he appeared only to remind me how much I reminded him of my mother—something he loathed. He never protected me from my stepfather, and I spent years longing for my father's love. Letting go of that fantasy cut deeper than I liked to admit.

My mother died by suicide when I was 23, left to grapple with the chaotic legacy of my upbringing. Part of me was angry at her for leaving me with our shared demons; another part understood she'd been drowning for years. And then, there was the quiet, ashamed part that felt relieved it was finally over.

In January 1987, grief and desperation collided, and I left Los Angeles for New York. I was chasing a vision of freedom, hoping physical distance might offer emotional distance as well. New York—frenetic, gritty, and unapologetically alive—matched the storm inside me. I tried new jobs. I was going to be an actress or a model—anything but me. But the problem with moving three thousand miles away was that I went with me. In that moment, I finally realized: You can't outrun pain.

By the end of 1989, I found myself returning to Los Angeles. I was holding on to an ex-boyfriend's promise of reunion, but that failed before we even got a second date. Facing the city I had fled felt like personal defeat. Fear of failure loomed large, but maybe that fear fueled my resilience. I had survived before—leaving home, moving to New York—and I figured I could do it again.

Sometimes, that's exactly what resilience is: doing the hard thing, even when you feel like you can't, and showing up anyway. I don't regret that leap of faith. Sometimes you have to leave the soil that's suffocating you to see how deep your roots can grow. New York showed me I was more than my pain—even if I still carried the trauma in my bones.

Even with that taste of independence, I wasn't free from my past. I may have been a married woman, but I was still living with guilt over my mother's death and my brother being in prison. I was still craving my father's love and acceptance. The stress of daily life—raising children, financial strains, an unsteady marriage—piled on top of buried pain. Pills offered an escape, initially under the guise of pain management, but soon they became my emotional crutch.

I told myself I was still functioning: I was there for my kids (or so I thought), paid bills, and appeared "normal" enough on the outside.

But inside, old wounds festered. The vow I'd made (don't become your mother) dissolved under the weight of denial. Unless you've walked the path of unrelenting pain, it's hard to grasp how tempting numbness can be.

My rock bottom wasn't a dramatic crash; it was a slow, suffocating realization that I had edged too close to the person I'd vowed never to be. I saw wreckage in my relationships, finances, and the lies I'd told to keep using. I had a choice: sink or claw my way out.

To stand a chance at recovery, I had to let go of two obsessions: waiting for my father's approval and trying to understand why my mother gave up on life. I couldn't alter the past or resurrect someone else's capacity to love me. Letting go of that longing broke my heart, but it also freed me.

My father died on April Fool's Day 2018, without ever giving me the validation I craved. He even made sure I was excluded from his funeral. Cruel as that was, I eventually found a grim sort of cosmic joke in it—he was a fool for not loving me. It was a sobering reminder that some losses never tie up neatly. Yet, I also felt an odd sense of release. With him gone, I no longer had to hope for words he would never say.

In therapy afterward, a counselor told me, "You don't have to prove anything anymore," and I realized how much of my identity had been wrapped up in trying to justify my existence. Those words freed me to live for me, not just in reaction to the people who'd hurt me.

By this point, I understood that resilience is not a neat, triumphant arc. It's the daily act of showing up—even when you're exhausted, even when you hate yourself for past mistakes, even when the world says you should have failed long ago. It's letting yourself believe in a future that isn't determined solely by what happened to you.

When my husband and I split and later reconciled, it was another test of perseverance. We tore open old wounds and asked hard questions about whether love could be salvaged beneath all the pain. Sometimes, resilience means leaving; sometimes, it means staying and fighting for what can be rebuilt. For us, that fight was worth it.

For as long as I can remember, I've wanted to be a writer—to take the chaos of my life and shape it into something that might speak to others who've felt lost or broken. As I near 63, I'm stepping into that dream, writing my story so it can finally serve a purpose beyond my own healing. There's power in putting words to things you once only whispered in a therapist's office. It's an act of reclaiming my voice.

I also volunteer with Hadassah, an organization that feels like an antidote to the isolation and shame of my past. Advocating for others has become a source of renewal for me—a chance to transform the pain I once carried in silence into action that helps build community and wellness.

My brother is still caught in heroin's grip—a tether to a past I sometimes long to leave behind. But I've learned the difference between healthy support and enabling, and I try to show him compassion without sacrificing myself.

Meanwhile, I do my best to mend relationships with my children, proving daily that I'm no longer the mother who disappears behind pills. Resilience isn't a milestone you cross; it's a practice woven into everyday living. It's each hard conversation you stay present for, each boundary you enforce, each morning you wake up and choose not to give up on yourself. Healing doesn't follow a neat schedule; it happens slowly, with setbacks and breakthroughs intertwined.

Approaching 63, my life is far from perfect, but it's more authentic than ever. I've learned that resilience is as much about gentleness as it is about strength—gentleness with our own scars, gentleness with our slower-than-we'd-like progress, gentleness in how we forgive ourselves for surviving any way we knew how.

If there's one thing my story reveals, it's that resilience often hides in the unremarkable moments—when you choose not to use it, when you let yourself cry but still get out of bed, when you apologize, set a boundary, or speak a truth you used to bury. It's not about being unbreakable. It's about deciding that even broken pieces can be reassembled into something worthy and strong.

You don't need anyone's permission or approval to believe in your own future. You don't have to wait for a dramatic rock bottom or for a parent to finally say, "I love you." You are allowed to heal right now, exactly as you are. Yes, it will be messy. Sometimes, you'll slip back into old habits or doubt your progress. But each time you choose to keep going, you're practicing resilience.

So, here I stand with a heart that's been battered but not destroyed. Every piece of my journey, even the bitter ones, has taught me that resilience is less about bouncing back and more about deciding to continue, no matter how many times you stumble. And in that deciding, there is a quiet, extraordinary power.

Wherever you are in your story, remember: You are enough. You've always been enough. You can rewrite your life, chapter by chapter, in whatever way leads you towards healing and wholeness. That's what I've done—and what I'll keep doing, every single day that I get to be alive.

Lovely LaGuerre

Founder and CEO of Pure Heavenly Hair, LLC

https://www.twitter.com/Heavenly_Pure
https://www.facebook.com/pureheavenlyhairboutique
https://instagram.com/pureheavenlyhair
Pure Heavenly Hair and Beauty
https://pureheavenlyhair.com/
Commercial and Luxury Real Estate
https://lovelysellsvegas.com/

ABOUT PURE HEAVENLY HAIR & BEAUTY

At Pure Heavenly Hair and Beauty our commitment to inclusivity and individuality is at the heart of everything we do. We celebrate all forms of beauty backgrounds, understanding that each person's journey is unique. Whether it's through our deeply moisturizing lip oils that enhance your natural glow or our go to wigs hair collections that bring life back to your locks, Pure Heavenly is here to honor and elevate your essence in every way. What truly makes us different is our belief in the power of connections with others. When you choose Pure Heavenly Hair and Beauty, you're choosing more than just a brand. You're embracing a lifestyle of conscious beauty, where every product is a ritual, every application a moment of self-care, and every result a testament to the heavenly within you. Come Unleash Your Beauty From Within! Join us in our mission to redefine your beauty purely, naturally, and beautifully. Experience the heavenly touch of our products and discover what it means to truly elevate your essence with Pure Heavenly Hair and Beauty! Pure Beauty | Pure Confidence | Purely Heavenly You!

Resilience in Her Cup: Brewing Dreams Into Legacy

By Lovely LaGuerre

I Never Meant to Follow Trends, I Came to Redefine Them

My journey in the beauty industry didn't begin with a glamorous launch or a shiny office. It started in quiet, personal moments, the kind where dreams whisper louder than fear, and your heart tells you there's something more for you to build. I didn't step into this space to just sell beauty. I came to help women feel whole, to remind them they are seen, powerful, and worthy beyond the mirror.

I wasn't chasing a trend. I was chasing transformation.

From Dreaming to Doing

Before the clients, before the shop, before the praise, it was just me and a vision. A woman with a burning desire to build something that mattered. Not just lipsticks or lashes. Something that would help another woman look at herself and finally say, "There I am. I remember her."

I didn't have investors. I didn't come from money. I didn't have a blueprint. But what I did have was heart. A fierce belief that my vision and the women I was called to serve were worth fighting for.

So, I pulled out my laptop, grabbed a notebook, and went to work. I stayed up late researching ingredients, sketching branding ideas, and figuring out fulfillment with no team, no map, just pure determination.

Finding Myself Again

Along the way, I started finding pieces of myself I didn't know I had lost: the fearless little girl who dreamed without limits, the teenager who loved making others feel beautiful, and the woman who once doubted if she was enough but kept showing up anyway.

That's when it clicked, I wasn't just building a brand. I was reclaiming my identity.

Every choice, every launch, every word I wrote started reflecting the woman I was becoming: bold, brave, and deeply rooted in purpose. I began hearing from customers who wore my products to job interviews, weddings, on tough days, and at turning points. They didn't just feel beautiful, they felt empowered.

That's the moment I realized: Beauty with soul has the power to heal.

The Grit Behind the Glam

People often see the highlight reel: the polished website, the pretty packaging. But they don't see what it took to get here.

They don't see the moments of betrayal, the partnerships that fell apart right before launch, or the heartbreak that made me question if I was really cut out for this. They don't see the nights I cried quietly after pouring everything into something that didn't work out.

But through it all, I learned that resilience isn't about being unbreakable; it's about letting yourself fall, then choosing to rise again, wiser and stronger.

Behind every polished photo was a night filled with doubt. Behind every selling product, there was a message of a thousand small victories: choosing faith over fear, choosing to keep going when quitting felt easier.

I had to pause. Rebuild. Set boundaries. Find balance. This time, I built slower. But I built better.

Not Just a Brand, A Safe Place

I've learned that hustle without healing is a fast track to burnout. That "boss babe" culture doesn't tell the whole story. I asked myself: What's the point of building a throne if I'm too tired to sit on it.

So, I slowed down and got intentional. I made joy a non-negotiable. I blocked out space for rest. I surrounded myself with women who didn't just cheer for my wins; they saw my weariness and didn't judge it.

I infused that same energy into my brand. I didn't just want to create products, I wanted to create a space. A space where women felt safe to be themselves. A space where softness was strength, and where showing up even when tired was still powerful.

This brand became a reflection of my soul: a blend of boldness, softness, sisterhood, and truth.

Purpose Over Product

As we grew, I made a promise to myself that this would never just be about selling. It would always be about serving.

Every product I created came with a deeper message: "You are enough." Every campaign was an invitation to show up fully. Every word I shared came from a place of truth and transparency.

I wasn't just selling lashes or lipstick. I was building a legacy.

I started asking bigger questions. How can I use my platform to shift the narrative? How do I create a brand that reminds women they don't need to shrink to be accepted?

And the answer came clearly: by living out loud. By telling the truth. By creating something beautiful, not just to look at, but to live through.

My goal was never just to build a brand. It was to build a movement.

The Beauty in Becoming

Looking back, I realize the real success wasn't just in the sales. It was in the becoming the woman I used to need.

And if I can become her, so can you.

To every woman reading this: I see you. I know what it feels like to carry big dreams in a world that tries to box you in. But let this be your reminder: You don't need permission. You are the permission.

You don't have to wait until you have it all figured out. Just start. Even if your hands are shaking, start anyway.

Your story is your strength. Your softness is your power. Your vision is valid.

So, What's Next?

I'm far from finished.

I'm expanding. Creating courses to help other beautypreneurs rise. Hosting my podcast that pours into women who are ready to rebuild, reclaim, and rise. Collaborating with change-makers who believe that beauty is about more than looks; it's about legacy.

Because I didn't just come to make noise. I came to make history.

And to the woman who's still wondering if she can do this, I say: You already have everything you need. Just start. Trust your pour.

Because within your cup of resilience lies the power to shift not just your world but the worlds of every woman watching you.

Becoming the Woman I Needed

As I kept growing through the highs, the heartbreaks, and the hustle, I started noticing something. The women who showed up around me? They weren't just customers. They were mirrors. They saw pieces of their own stories in mine. And that's when it hit me: I wasn't here just to sell products, I was here to pour into people.

I began sharing my stories, not because I had all the answers, but because I knew the power of sharing the journey, unfiltered and real. I let people into the messy middle, the behind-the-scenes, the moments I questioned if I was really cut out for this. And slowly, I started seeing how every step forward was part of something bigger.

I believe in community over competition, truly. I've sat in rooms where power was held tightly, and I've also built rooms where it's shared freely. I hold the mic, and then I pass it. I walk through doors and make sure they stay open behind me. Because legacy? It doesn't grow in isolation; it's built in connection.

More Than Beauty: It's a Movement

What started as a small vision has evolved into something deeper: a movement, a message, a way of life. To me, beauty isn't about exclusivity; it's for every woman who dares to own her truth and shine unapologetically.

Each product I create is more than a beauty item; it's a reminder. A bold red lip that whispers courage. Hair extensions that feel like a form of therapy. These aren't just things we wear; they're tools that help us see and feel ourselves again.

The feedback has been well received in the best way, women sharing how my creations made them feel seen, brave, and beautiful. That's the fuel that keeps me going.

And as things grew, so did my dreams. Looking to expand my brand, and I've got haircare on the way, products made to nourish not just your strands, but your spirit, too.

I've spoken on stages I once dreamed of, not to deliver polished speeches, but to share real stories. Because women deserve to know:

greatness doesn't mean perfection. It means showing up, scars and all.

Legacy, I've realized, isn't about something you leave behind. It's how you live today with intention, honesty, and heart. Every decision I make, every bold move I take—it's all part of that.

My Goal? To Be Felt, Not Just Seen

I don't just want recognition, I want resonance. I want my story to sit in someone's spirit and whisper, "You can do this, too." Whether she's reading in her journal, sitting in a boardroom, or getting ready in front of a mirror, I want her to feel it.

When I look ahead, I see so much more than profit. I see platforms, spaces that nourish, educate, and empower. I imagine retreats, beauty lounges, podcast studios, writing circles, all places where women can gather, be real, and leave changed.

And it's not about me being the loudest in the room. It's about creating the room.

Because when women build together, what we build lasts.

A Cup of Resilience for the Next Generation

To the younger generation watching us, I want to give you more than inspiration. I want to leave you with tools, truth, and wisdom. Real talk: Beauty isn't about perfection, it's about power. And business? It should fuel your peace, not drain your soul. Legacy isn't far off in the distance; it's in the choices you make today.

Why I Keep Pouring

There are still tough days. I'd be lying if I said otherwise. Fear still visits sometimes, whispering doubts. But I've learned fear doesn't mean failure; it means I'm stretching.

I keep pouring because I know what's at stake. Women aren't just impacted by what I create; they're impacted by how I lead, what I share, and the values I stand on.

My story isn't mine alone. It belongs to every woman who's ever felt overlooked, underestimated, or overwhelmed. The more I share it, the more power we all reclaim.

So, I keep creating. I keep showing up. I walk into rooms I once felt unqualified for, because now I understand: My story is my qualification.

The Power of Your Pour

If you're reading this, hear me clearly: Your dreams matter. Your voice matters. And what you pour into the world? That matters more than you know.

Don't wait until everything feels perfect. Just start. Start messy. Start scared. Start unsure. Just start.

And don't ever forget your resilience isn't a flaw. It's your superpower.

Pour passion into your vision. Pour truth into your story. Pour faith into your next step. Because you're not just building a brand, you're building a beacon.

One Last Sip

My story is still unfolding page by page, pour by pour. And I'm grateful for every bit of it, the growth, the grace, the grit.

To the woman reading this who feels a little worn out: You don't have to be perfect to be powerful. You don't need to have it all together to be impactful. You don't need permission to lead, just a little courage.

So raise your cup, fill it with boldness, beauty, and belief, and go out there and share it.

Because the world doesn't just need your product. It needs you.

What's Next Is Now

I'm just getting started. I'm growing the line and creating spaces for beauty bosses to rise. Podcast platforms to share your voice, build with purpose, and collaborate with women who are in alignment.

This journey isn't just about me; it's about all of us. Every woman who needs to know: You can rise. You can rebuild. You can pour your own cup of resilience and declare with your whole chest, "I'm not done yet."

A Final Pour for You

To the woman still finding her footing: You don't need permission. You are the permission. You don't need it all figured out. You just need the next brave step.

Resilience isn't about never falling; it's about rising again and again, crown slightly tilted, soul still shining.

Your dream? It's still valid. Your voice? Still needed. Your story? Absolutely sacred.

So take your time. Brew your dreams slowly. Stir in faith. Sweeten it with strength. And then go serve the world with boldness and heart.

Because you're not just creating a business.

You're building a beacon.

You're not just a dreamer.

You're a doer.

And you're not just resilient.

You're revolutionary.

Raise your cup, queen, the world is waiting for what you carry.

JOIN THE MOVEMENT!
#BAUW

Becoming An Unstoppable Woman
With She Rises Studios

She Rises Studios was founded by Hanna Olivas and Adriana Luna Carlos, the mother-daughter duo, in mid-2020 as they saw a need to help empower women worldwide. They are the podcast hosts of the *She Rises Studios Podcast* and Amazon best-selling authors and motivational speakers who travel the world. Hanna and Adriana are the movement creators of #BAUW - Becoming An Unstoppable Woman: The movement has been created to universally impact women of all ages, at whatever stage of life, to overcome insecurities, and adversities, and develop an unstoppable mindset. She Rises Studios educates, celebrates, and empowers women globally.

Looking to Join Us in our Next Anthology or Publish YOUR Own?

She Rises Studios Publishing offers full-service publishing, marketing, book tour, and campaign services. For more information, contact info@sherisesstudios.com

We are always looking for women who want to share their stories and expertise and feature their businesses on our podcasts, in our books, and in our magazines.

SEE WHAT WE DO

OUR PODCAST	OUR BOOKS	OUR SERVICES

Be featured in the Becoming An Unstoppable Woman magazine, published in 13 countries and sold in all major retailers. Get the visibility you need to LEVEL UP in your business!

Have your own TV show streamed across major platforms like Roku TV, Amazon Fire Stick, Apple TV and more!

Learn to leverage your expertise. Build your online presence and grow your audience with FENIX TV.
https://fenixtv.sherisesstudios.com/

Visit www.SheRisesStudios.com to see how YOU can join the #BAUW movement and help your community to achieve the UNSTOPPABLE mindset.

Have you checked out the *She Rises Studios Podcast?*

Find us on all MAJOR platforms: Spotify, IHeartRadio, Apple Podcasts, Google Podcasts, etc.

Looking to become a sponsor or build a partnership?

Email us at info@sherisesstudios.com

SHE RISES
STUDIOS

www.ingramcontent.com/pod-product-compliance
Lightning Source LLC
Chambersburg PA
CBHW071020120626
46546CB00003B/1178